WALCH PUBLISHING

Daily Warm-Ups

LAW

Level II

Brad Lawwill

W9-DJM-481

The classroom teacher may reproduce materials in this book for classroom use only.
The reproduction of any part for an entire school or school system is strictly prohibited.
No part of this publication may be transmitted, stored, or recorded in any form
without written permission from the publisher.

1   2   3   4   5   6   7   8   9   10

ISBN 0-8251-5516-9

Copyright © 2005

J. Weston Walch, Publisher

P.O. Box 658 • Portland, Maine 04104-0658

walch.com

Printed in the United States of America

iii

Table of Contents

Introduction   iv

The *Daily Warm-Ups* series is a wonderful way to turn extra classroom minutes into valuable learning time. The 180 quick activities—one for each day of the school year—cover all aspects of law. They may be used at the beginning of class to get students focused, near the end of class to make good use of transitional time, in the middle of class to help students shift gears between lessons—or whenever you have minutes that now go unused. In addition to helping students warm up and focus, they are a natural lead-in to more in-depth activities.

Daily Warm-Ups are easy to use. Simply photocopy the day's activity and distribute it. Or make a transparency of the activity and project it on the board. You may want to use the activities for extra credit points or as a check on your students' critical-thinking skills as they are acquired and built over time.

However you choose to use them, *Daily Warm-Ups* are a convenient and useful supplement to your regular class lessons. Make every minute of your class time count!

Law in the United States

What Is the Law?

Laws are rules for conduct that are established by government. Citizens are required to follow these rules and face consequences if they fail to do so. The severity of the consequence depends on the nature of the law that they violate.

The first known set of laws is the Code of Hammurabi, which was compiled sometime between 1792 B.C.E. and 1750 B.C.E. when Hammurabi was the king of Babylon. The Code of Hammurabi lists 282 rules and consequences for a variety of actions. Included among these rules are the concepts of "an eye for an eye" ("If a man put out the eye of another man, his eye shall be put out") and "a tooth for a tooth" ("If a man knock out the teeth of his equal, his teeth shall be knocked out").

Why is it important for a society to have laws? Write two or three sentences for your answer.

Daily Warm-Ups: Law

© 2005 Walch Publishing

© 2005 Walch Publishing

2

Law in the United States

As the United States was declaring its independence from British rule, John Adams, a Massachusetts delegate to the Continental Congress, said, "We are a nation of laws and not men."

The early history of the United States demonstrates the emphasis placed on the law. One of the first acts of the founders was to create a supreme law of the land, the Articles of Confederation, in 1777. This document was eventually replaced with the current supreme law of the land, the U.S. Constitution, which was written in 1787.

What did John Adams mean when he said that the United States was "a nation of laws and not men"? Write two or three sentences for your answer.

Daily Warm-Ups: Law

© 2005 Walch Publishing

3

Law in the United States

The Articles of Confederation

The first document to draw the colonies together as a nation was known as "The Articles of Confederation and Perpetual Union" and was adopted by the Continental Congress in 1777.

This document established a federal government but gave it limited powers. The current United States government is comprised of three branches: the legislative branch to make laws; the executive branch to enforce laws; and the judicial branch to interpret laws. The Articles of Confederation merely established a legislative branch and gave the federal government no ability to enforce the laws against the individual states. The states maintained control over matters such as foreign affairs, defense, and public finances.

The limited power given to the federal government under the Articles of Confederation made it difficult to bring the states together as a united nation. Why would this be the case? Write two or three sentences for your answer.

Daily Warm-Ups: Law

4

The United States Constitution

In 1787, the Continental Congress gathered in Philadelphia for the express purpose of revising the Articles of Confederation. In the ten years since the Articles were adopted, it had become clear that a stronger central government was necessary. While the Articles of Confederation established only a legislative branch of government and reserved a great deal of power to the states, the U.S. Constitution created a legislative, an executive, and a judicial branch, each with its own set of powers. The powers established for each branch were intended to strengthen the role of the federal government, while ensuring that no one branch of government held too much power.

The U.S. Constitution is the oldest written constitution in the world. Part of why it is so enduring is a provision contained in Article V that allows for changes, or amendments, to be made to the document. Since its original adoption, the U.S. Constitution has been amended 27 times. Why is it important to allow for amendments? Write two or three sentences for your answer.

© 2005 Walch Publishing

© 2005 Walch Publishing

Law in the United States

The Bill of Rights

One of the early criticisms voiced by the state legislatures that were asked to approve the U.S. Constitution was that it did not contain a list of citizen's rights that were to be protected. The first United States Congress remedied this concern by creating such a list. This *Bill of Rights* was drafted by James Madison and was ratified, or approved, by the states in 1791. The Bill of Rights is contained in the first ten amendments of the U.S. Constitution.

Daily Warm-Ups: Law

You have just been selected to write a Bill of Rights for a newly formed government. What is one freedom or right that you will select to protect?

Why? Write two or three sentences for your answer.

© 2005 Walch Publishing

The Bill of Rights: The First Amendment (Religious and Political Freedom)

The First Amendment of the U.S. Constitution reads:

Congress shall make no law respecting an establishment of religion, or prohibiting the free exercise thereof; or abridging the freedom of speech, or of the press; or the right of the people peaceably to assemble, and to petition the Government for a redress of grievances.

What rights are protected by the First Amendment? Do you agree that all of these rights should be protected? Why or why not? Write two or three sentences to explain your opinion.

Daily Warm-Ups: Law

Law in the United States

The Bill of Rights: The Second Amendment (The Right to Bear Arms)

The Second Amendment of the U.S. Constitution states:

> A well regulated Militia, being necessary to the security of a free State, the right of the people to keep and bear Arms, shall not be infringed.

Daily Warm-Ups: Law

The exact meaning of the Second Amendment has led to a lot of debate. Some believe that it protects the right of American citizens to keep and bear arms. Others believe that it protects the right of American citizens to keep and bear arms, but only if they are part of a "well regulated Militia." What do you think and why? Write two or three sentences for your answer.

© 2005 Walch Publishing

8

The Bill of Rights: The Third Amendment (Quartering Soldiers)

The Third Amendment of the U.S. Constitution states:

> No Soldier shall, in time of peace be quartered in any house, without the consent of the Owner, nor in time of war, but in a manner to be prescribed by law.

The Third Amendment is intended to prevent the government from forcing homeowners to house soldiers during a time of peace. British soldiers were quartered in colonists' homes prior to the American Revolution. During a time of war, is quartering allowed? If so, under what conditions is it allowed? Write two or three sentences for your answer.

Daily Warm-Ups: Law

© 2005 Walch Publishing

The Bill of Rights: The Fourth Amendment (Unreasonable Searches and Seizures)

Daily Warm-Ups: Law

© 2005 Walch Publishing

The Fourth Amendment of the U.S. Constitution states:

> The right of the people to be secure in their persons, houses, papers, and effects, against unreasonable searches and seizures, shall not be violated, and no Warrants shall issue, but upon probable cause, supported by Oath or affirmation, and particularly describing the place to be searched, and the persons or things to be seized.

The Fourth Amendment protects an individual's right to privacy by prohibiting the government from conducting unreasonable searches and seizures.

A local jewelry store is robbed, and the police suspect that Alyssa has committed the crime. However, they have no evidence to support their suspicion. The following morning, they wait for Alyssa to go to work and then let themselves into her home to look for the stolen jewels. Are the police allowed to do this? Why or why not? Write two or three sentences for your answer.

The Bill of Rights: The Fifth Amendment (Due Process and Just Compensation)

The Fifth Amendment of the U.S. Constitution reads:

No person shall be held to answer for a capital, or otherwise infamous crime, unless on a presentment or indictment of a Grand Jury, except in cases arising in the land or naval forces, or in the Militia, when in actual service in time of War or public danger; nor shall any person be subject for the same offence to be twice put in jeopardy of life or limb; nor shall be compelled in any criminal case to be a witness against himself, nor be deprived of life, liberty, or property, without due process of law; nor shall private property be taken for public use, without just compensation.

The ability of the government to take an individual's private property for public use is known as "eminent domain." Does the Fifth Amendment provide any protection to citizens with respect to "eminent domain"? Write two or three sentences for your answer.

© 2005 Walch Publishing

© 2005 Walch Publishing

The Bill of Rights: The Sixth Amendment (Rights of the Accused)

The Sixth Amendment of the U.S. Constitution states:

> In all criminal prosecutions, the accused shall enjoy the right to a speedy and public trial, by an impartial jury of the State and district wherein the crime shall have been committed, which district shall have been previously ascertained by law, and to be informed of the nature and cause of the accusation; to be confronted with the witnesses against him; to have compulsory process for obtaining witnesses in his favor, and to have the Assistance of Counsel for his defense.

In the landmark case *Miranda v. Arizona*, the Supreme Court ruled that a person in custody cannot be questioned by police until he or she has been told that, if he or she cannot afford an attorney, one will be provided at no cost. How is this different from the Sixth Amendment right to have assistance of counsel? Write two or three sentences for your answer.

Daily Warm-Ups: Law

© 2005 Walch Publishing

The Bill of Rights: The Seventh Amendment (Trial by Jury in Civil Cases)

The Seventh Amendment of the U.S. Constitution states:

In suits at common law, where the value in controversy shall exceed twenty dollars, the right of trial by jury shall be preserved, and no fact tried by a jury, shall be otherwise reexamined in any Court of the United States, than according to the rules of the common law.

One of the most popular demands by those states who called for a bill of rights was the protection of the right to trial by jury. This right to a trial by a jury of fellow citizens instead of a trial by a judge (who is a member of government) was seen as a very important measure to protect against tyranny. Why? Write two or three sentences for your answer.

Daily Warm-Ups: Law

The Bill of Rights: The Eighth Amendment (Bail and Punishment)

The Eighth Amendment of the U.S. Constitution states:

Excessive bail shall not be required, nor excessive fines imposed, nor cruel and unusual punishments inflicted.

The Eighth Amendment forbids the imposition of "cruel and unusual punishments." Some states still allow the death penalty, or capital punishment, when people who are convicted of very severe crimes (such as murder) are put to death by the government. Do you think that the death penalty is "cruel and unusual"? Why or why not? Write two or three sentences to explain your opinion.

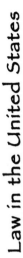

Daily Warm-Ups: Law

© 2005 Walch Publishing

13

The Bill of Rights: The Ninth Amendment (Rights Retained by People)

The Ninth Amendment of the U.S. Constitution states:

The enumeration in the Constitution, of certain rights, shall not be construed to deny or disparage others retained by the people.

When debating whether or not to add a bill of rights to the U.S. Constitution, some argued that providing a list of rights may lead the government to contend that those were the only rights held by the people. What is the purpose of the Ninth Amendment? Write two or three sentences for your answer.

© 2005 Walch Publishing

14

Daily Warm-Ups: Law

The Bill of Rights: The Tenth Amendment (Powers Reserved to States or People)

The Tenth Amendment of the U.S. Constitution states:

> The powers not delegated to the United States by the Constitution, nor prohibited by it to the States, are reserved to the States respectively, or to the people.

Daily Warm-Ups: Law

The purpose of the Tenth Amendment is to make it clear that the powers not delegated to the federal government in the U.S. Constitution are reserved to the states and to the citizens of the United States. Why do you think it was important to the drafters of the Bill of Rights that these powers be reserved to the states and to the people? Write two or three sentences for your answer.

© 2005 Walch Publishing

15

16

The Bill of Rights: Matching

Match the number of the constitutional amendment on the left with the individual right that it protects on the right.

Amendment	Individual Right
Fourth	the right to be protected against excessive bail
First	the right to be protected against unreasonable searches and seizures
Eighth	freedom of religion
Fifth	the right to due process of law

© 2005 Walch Publishing

Law in the United States

The Reserved Powers Clause

In contrast to the Tenth Amendment, which stands for the proposition that all powers not delegated to the federal government are reserved to the states and the people, Article 1, Section 8 of the U.S. Constitution sets forth the powers specifically delegated to the federal government. Among them, the federal government has the exclusive authority to "provide for the common defense," "regulate commerce with foreign nations," "coin money," "declare war," and "raise and support armies." In addition, Article I, Section 10 of the U.S. Constitution sets forth activities that cannot be conducted by the states. Among them, the states are prohibited from coining money, entering into treaties, and declaring war.

Following a hockey game in which the Toronto Maple Leafs beat the Detroit Red Wings by a score of 4–3, the state of Michigan declares war on Canada. Is this allowed or prohibited by the U.S. Constitution? Write two or three sentences for your answer.

17

© 2005 *Walch* Publishing

© 2005 Walch Publishing

Law in the United States

State Law

Each state has its own set of laws, typically referred to as statutes, that establish rules of conduct in those areas in which power has not been exclusively granted to the federal government.

State laws generally address such things as

- the authority of local governments (such as cities, towns, and counties)
- rules of conduct for certain businesses and professions (including the practice of law or medicine)
- family law (such as marriage, divorce, and child custody)
- criminal laws and procedures

Provide an example of a law that may be different from one state to another.

Daily Warm-Ups: Law

Law in the United States

Local Government

Within each state, local government bodies, such as cities, towns, and counties, have the power to create their own laws. These laws are typically referred to as ordinances. That power is defined by state statute and, similarly to the Reserved Powers clause of the Tenth Amendment, is generally limited to those powers that are not granted exclusively to the state.

In what county and town do you live? What are some ordinances in your town or county? Give two or three examples.

Daily Warm-Ups: Law

© 2005 Walch Publishing

19

Separation of Powers

The drafters of the U.S. Constitution did not want to create a federal government that was so strong that it overrode the will of the states and the people. To accomplish this, the U.S. Constitution established three branches of the federal government—the legislative branch, the executive branch, and the judicial branch—each with its own powers and the ability to "check" the power of the other two branches. This separation of powers creates a system of "checks and balances" that prevents any one branch of government from having too much power or influence.

Match the power on the left with the branch of government to which it belongs on the right.

Power

to make laws

to declare law unconstitutional or invalid

to appoint judges and certain governmental officials

Branch of Government

judicial

legislative

executive

© 2005 Walch Publishing

Daily Warm-Ups: Law

The Legislative Branch

The legislative branch of the United States government is known as Congress. The United States Congress is bicameral in nature. This means that there are two lawmaking groups, or assemblies. These assemblies are the House of Representatives and the Senate. A member of the House of Representatives is called a congressman or congresswoman. A member of the Senate is called a senator.

The House of Representatives has proportional representation—each state has voting power in accordance with the size of its population. In the Senate, a fixed number of representatives (currently 2) for each state is allowed, regardless of the size of the state.

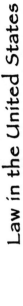

Daily Warm-Ups: Law

In the U.S. House of Representatives, the state of Maine has 2 representatives and the state of California has 53 representatives. Does this make sense to you? Why or why not? Write two or three sentences for your answer.

21

© 2005 Walch Publishing

The Executive Branch

© 2005 Walch Publishing

The executive branch, led by the president of the United States, is responsible for enforcing the laws made by the legislative branch. In addition, the president has limited legislative powers. When a bill is approved by Congress, the president can do one of three things. He or she can sign it into law, veto (or reject) it, or do nothing with it. If he or she does nothing with it and Congress is still in session, the bill becomes law. If Congress is no longer in session, the bill dies. This situation is known as the *pocket veto*.

The president may only veto a bill in its entirety. He or she may not choose portions of the bill to veto. The ability to veto portions of a bill is known as a *line-item veto*.

Congress passes an environmental law that forces the automotive and airline industries to manufacture only engines that meet strict air pollution criteria. The bill comes to the president, and he or she decides to veto only those portions of the bill that relate to the airline industry. Can the president do that? Write two or three sentences for your answer.

Daily Warm-Ups: Law

The Judicial Branch: Federal Courts

The judicial branch is responsible for interpreting laws and evaluating conduct in the context of those laws. The courts have the power of judicial review. This is the power to review (and potentially reverse) the decisions and actions of the legislative and executive branches of government. The federal courts are made up of the United States Supreme Court (the highest court in the country), 94 United States District Courts that hold civil and criminal trials, 13 United States Courts of Appeals that hear appeals (a request to review a judgment) from the United States District Courts and from decisions of federal administrative agencies, and the United States Bankruptcy Courts, which have exclusive jurisdiction over bankruptcy cases because these cases cannot be filed in state court.

Bernie decides that he can no longer handle his debt and decides to declare bankruptcy. He goes to the state court in his county and tries to file for bankruptcy, but the state court refuses to accept the case. Why? Write two or three sentences for your answer.

Daily Warm-Ups: Law

23

© 2005 *Walch* Publishing

The Judicial Branch: State Courts

Each state has its own judicial system that hears nonfederal cases. The exact composition of these judicial systems varies from state to state but generally includes the following three levels:

- Trial courts, which are the first courts to hear a case. Often, states will establish specialized trial courts to hear cases related to a certain subject matter, such as probate courts to hear matters related to wills and estates, and family courts to hear matters related to divorce and child custody.

- Courts of appeal, which review the judgments of the trial courts.

- A state supreme court, which is the highest appellate court in the state. Generally speaking, decisions of a state's supreme court can be appealed to a federal court of appeals and, ultimately, the United States Supreme Court.

What is the power of judicial review? How does judicial review act as a check against the power of the legislative and executive branches of government? Write two or three sentences for your answer.

Daily Warm-Ups: Law

© 2005 Walch Publishing

The U.S. Supreme Court: Article III

The first section of Article III of the U.S. Constitution established that the federal judicial power of the United States would rest with "one supreme Court, and in such inferior Courts as the Congress may from time to time ordain and establish."

Based on this provision, the United States Supreme Court was created in 1789 and was organized in February of 1790.

The Court is comprised of one Chief Justice and associate justices. The number of associate justices is determined by Congress and is currently at eight. Justices are appointed by the president of the United States and must be approved by the Senate. Each justice is appointed for life and can only be removed by death, resignation, or impeachment.

What, if any, effect does the election of the president of the United States have on the Supreme Court? Write two or three sentences for your answer.

Daily Warm-Ups: Law

25

© 2005 Walch Publishing

© 2005 Walch Publishing

The U.S. Supreme Court: Jurisdiction

26

The authority of a court to be the first court to hear a case and to render a judgment is referred to as *original jurisdiction*, which can be either exclusive or concurrent. The U.S. Supreme Court has *exclusive jurisdiction* over cases in which a state is a party. This means that the U.S. Supreme Court is the only court with authority to try such a case. The U.S. Supreme Court has *concurrent jurisdiction* (or shared jurisdiction) with the lower federal courts on all cases affecting ambassadors, public ministers, and consuls.

The states of New Hampshire and Maine are involved in a disagreement over the location of the southern boundary between them. The state of New Hampshire believes that the entire Piscataqua River and all of Portsmouth Harbor belong to it. The state of Maine believes that the border is in the middle of the Piscataqua River. The state of New Hampshire decides to file a lawsuit against the state of Maine to resolve the issue. In what court should New Hampshire file its lawsuit? Why? Write two or three sentences for your answer.

Law in the United States

The U.S. Supreme Court: Writ of Certiorari

The authority of a court to review and change the decision of a lower court is known as *appellate jurisdiction*. The U.S. Supreme Court has limited appellate jurisdiction. Cases that come to the U.S. Supreme Court for appeal can arrive in one of two ways. First, a case can come by a *writ of certiorari* (*certiorari* is Latin for "to be informed of").

These are cases from federal courts of appeal or state courts when either the constitutionality of a law or treaty is in issue or a state law allegedly violates a federal law. The U.S. Supreme Court decides whether it will hear a case that arrives by certiorari. Second, the U.S. Supreme Court hears cases that come from three-judge federal district court panels.

After losing a lawsuit against the Federal Communications Commission, a major telecommunications company files a writ of certiorari asking the U.S. Supreme Court to review the case. Does the U.S. Supreme Court have to take the case? Why or why not? Write two or three sentences for your answer.

Daily Warm-Ups: Law

27

© 2005 *Walch* Publishing

The U.S. Supreme Court: Matching

Match the U.S. Supreme Court case on the left with its landmark ruling on the right.

Supreme Court Case

Marbury v. Madison (1803)

Roe v. Wade (1973)

Brown v. Board of Education (1954)

Texas v. Johnson (1989)

Bush v. Gore (2000)

Ruling

Racial segregation in public schools is unconstitutional.

The U.S. Supreme Court may review and invalidate laws if they are unconstitutional.

Flag burning is "symbolic speech" that is protected by the First Amendment.

The Florida State Supreme Court's order to recount presidential ballots was unconstitutional.

A woman's right to an abortion is a privacy right protected by the Fourteenth Amendment.

Daily Warm-Ups: Law

© 2005 Walch Publishing

28

Law in the United States

Areas of the Law

A person who practices law is called either an attorney or a lawyer. Lawyers may have a specialized practice, in which they work in just one subject matter, or they may have a more generalized practice, in which they work in more than one subject matter. Legal practice is broken up into many different areas, including criminal law and procedure, contract law, tort law, intellectual property law, family law, and bankruptcy law.

Daily Warm-Ups: Law

If you were to become a lawyer, in which of the above areas do you think you would like to practice? Why? Write two or three sentences for your answer.

© 2005 Walch Publishing

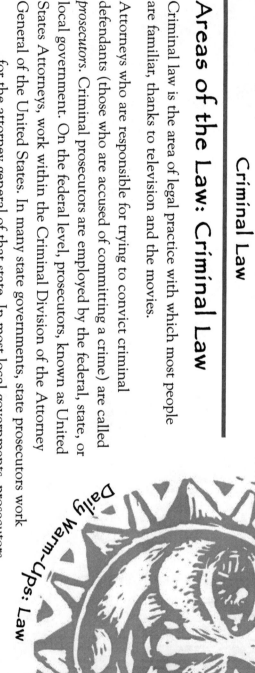

Areas of the Law: Criminal Law

Criminal law is the area of legal practice with which most people are familiar, thanks to television and the movies.

Attorneys who are responsible for trying to convict criminal defendants (those who are accused of committing a crime) are called *prosecutors*. Criminal prosecutors are employed by the federal, state, or local government. On the federal level, prosecutors, known as United States Attorneys, work within the Criminal Division of the Attorney General of the United States. In many state governments, state prosecutors work for the attorney general of that state. In most local governments, prosecutors work for an agency that is known as either the Office of the District Attorney or Office of the State's Attorney.

Imagine that you work as a prosecutor. What do you think you would like about that job? What do you think you would not like? Write two or three sentences for your answer.

Daily Warm-Ups: Law

© 2005 Walch Publishing

30

Criminal Law

Defense Attorneys

Attorneys who defend people accused of a crime are called *criminal defense attorneys*. Most local governments have an Office of the Public Defender. Attorneys who work for the public defender are generally assigned to represent accused criminal defendants who are indigent, which means they cannot afford a lawyer. If a local government does not have an Office of the Public Defender or if that office has too much criminal defense work for its lawyers to handle, criminal trial judges will assign private attorneys to handle the cases *pro bono*. *Pro bono* is a Latin phrase meaning "for the good." It describes legal work that is free.

If a criminal defendant cannot afford a lawyer, why does the government provide one at no cost? Write two or three sentences for your answer.

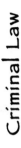

Daily Warm-Ups: Law

Jurisdiction

If a state's criminal law is violated, the criminal case will be tried in that state's judicial system. In a case involving criminal activity in multiple states, a state will have jurisdiction over that case if any criminal act was committed in that state; a criminal act committed outside of that state causes harm in that state; a criminal act was committed outside of that state, but an attempt to commit the crime or a conspiracy to commit the crime happened inside that state; or the crime involved an act or omission (failure to act) that constituted the neglect of a duty imposed by that state's law.

Kerry and three of his friends are vacationing in Michigan. While there, they plot to abduct Victor when they get home to Ohio. Three days later, while Kerry and his friends are in Wisconsin, they see Victor and abduct him right there. In what state or states can Kerry and his friends be tried for kidnapping? Write two or three sentences for your answer.

32

© 2005 Walch Publishing

Criminal Law

Categories of Crimes

Crimes are classified as felonies, misdemeanors, or infractions. An *infraction* is less serious than a misdemeanor and is usually punishable by a small fine. Examples of infractions would include parking tickets and jaywalking. A *misdemeanor* is a less serious crime than a felony and is usually punishable by a fine of not more than $2,500 or by imprisonment of not more than one year. Examples of misdemeanors include trespassing and reckless driving. A *felony* is a more serious crime than a misdemeanor. It is punishable by imprisonment of more than one year. In 38 states, the most serious felonies are punishable by death. Examples of felonies include murder, arson, aggravated assault, and driving under the influence.

Donell is stopped by police in Delaware for driving 65 miles per hour in a 30 mile per hour zone. Under Delaware law, reckless driving is defined to include exceeding the speed limit by more than 20 miles per hour. Has Donell committed an infraction, a misdemeanor, or a felony? What punishment might he receive? Write two or three sentences for your answer.

Daily Warm-Ups: Law

© 2005 Walch Publishing

Burden of Proof

In a criminal trial, a defendant is presumed innocent until proven guilty. To be convicted of a misdemeanor or a felony, the prosecutor must prove to the jury "beyond a reasonable doubt" that the defendant committed the crime. This requirement is called the *burden of proof.*

What do you think *beyond a reasonable doubt* means? How difficult do you think it is to meet this burden of proof? Write two or three sentences for your answer.

© 2005 Walch Publishing

© 2005 Walch Publishing

Criminal Law

Elements of a Crime

A crime involves two things:

- A voluntary physical act, which in Latin is called *actus reus*, or "guilty act"

- A mental state, which in Latin is called *mens rea*, or "guilty mind"

In order for a crime to have been committed, both the physical act and the mental state must be present at the same time.

Daily Warm-Ups: Law

Bobby is angry with a coworker, Ivan. Bobby decides to drive back to the office and hit Ivan in the head with a big rock. Hitting Ivan in the head with a rock would be considered battery, which is a criminal act. Because he intends to hit Ivan in the head with the rock for the purpose of harming him, Bobby has the required mental state for a crime. On the way to the office, Bobby runs over a small rock that shoots out from under his tire and accidentally hits Ivan in the head. Did Bobby commit a crime? Write two or three sentences for your answer.

Categories of Crimes

There are four principal categories of crimes. They are

- crimes against the person
- crimes against personal property
- crimes against the home or dwelling
- crimes against the judicial system

Name at least one crime that you think would fall within each of the four categories.

© 2005 Walch Publishing

36

Daily Warm-Ups: Law

Crimes Against the Person: Assault and Battery

Assault and *battery* are often mentioned together, but they are in fact two separate crimes.

Battery is a nonconsensual, intentional, or wrongful physical contact with a person that results in injury or an otherwise offensive touching. The physical contact does not need to be applied directly for it to constitute battery. For instance, if you cause your pit bull to bite the victim, you have committed a battery without actually touching the victim yourself. A battery that causes a serious injury that is committed with a deadly weapon or is committed by an adult male against a child, a woman, or a police officer is considered *aggravated battery* and is punishable by a longer prison term.

Carlos is shopping in a grocery store, trips over his shoelaces and knocks a display of soda cans onto an eight-year-old girl, causing a bump on her head. Has Carlos committed a battery, an aggravated battery, or no crime at all? Write two or three sentences for your answer.

Daily Warm-Ups: Law

© 2005 *Walch* Publishing

37

Crimes Against the Person: Assault

Assault is either an attempted battery, or a willful threat to inflict injury on someone, coupled with an apparent ability to inflict the injury. For criminal assault to occur, the victim must have a reasonable apprehension that he or she is going to be harmed in the immediate future.

Jack is in Denver and Mike is in Boston. During a heated phone conversation, Jack tells Mike, "When I fly home to Boston next month, I want you to meet me at Logan Airport so I can punch you in the face." Has Jack committed assault? Why or why not? Write two or three sentences for your answer.

© 2005 Walch Publishing

Daily Warm-Ups: Law

© 2005 *Walch Publishing*

Criminal Law

Crimes Against the Person: Criminal Homicide

Criminal homicide is the purposeful, knowing, reckless, or negligent killing of another person. If the killing of another person is done while carrying out a sentence of capital punishment, is done in war, is done in self-defense, or is done because it is the only way to restrain or capture an escaping felon, it is homicide, but it is not a crime.

Criminal homicide is divided into three categories: murder, voluntary manslaughter, and involuntary manslaughter. Murder is the most serious form of criminal homicide. Voluntary manslaughter is less serious than murder and more serious than involuntary manslaughter.

Daily Warm-Ups: Law

Max has been sentenced to die by lethal injection. At the time that his sentence is to be carried out, Jay is the person who inserts the poison into Max's arm, causing his death. Has Jay committed an act of homicide? Write two or three sentences for your answer.

Crimes Against the Person: Murder

Murder is the unlawful killing of another person if it is done with malice aforethought.

Malice aforethought exists if the killing was committed with the presence of one of the following states of mind:

* intent to kill
* intent to inflict great bodily injury
* intent to commit a dangerous felony (arson, rape, burglary)
* intent to act with reckless indifference or disregard to the possible consequences to human life

Ana finds an abandoned building in town and decides to set fire to it. Unbeknownst to Ana, Kirk is inside the building. Kirk is killed when the building burns to the ground. Has Ana committed murder? Write two or three sentences for your answer.

40

© 2005 Walch Publishing

Crimes Against the Person: Voluntary Manslaughter

Voluntary manslaughter is murder that has been provoked. The key to determining whether a killing is murder or voluntary manslaughter is determining the sufficiency of the provocation.

Provocation is sufficient to reduce murder to voluntary manslaughter if all of the following conditions are met:

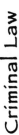

- The defendant was, in fact, provoked.

- The provocation created a "sudden and intense passion" that would cause "a reasonable person" to be provoked.

- There was not enough time for "a reasonable person" to calm down.

- The criminal defendant did not, in fact, calm down.

Describe a scenario in which you think a murder charge might be reduced to voluntary manslaughter. Write two or three sentences for your answer.

© 2005 Walch Publishing

Crimes Against the Person: Involuntary Manslaughter

Involuntary manslaughter is the killing of another that results from negligence or from the commission of an unlawful act (other than a dangerous felony). *Negligence* occurs when someone is doing something that he or she is legally allowed to do, but is doing it without an adequate amount of caution or without the required amount of skill.

Charlie is a carpenter and is renovating an apartment in a four-unit apartment complex. He has hired an electrician to do some wiring, but the electrician is late.

Charlie decides not to wait and does the wiring himself, even though he has no training in wiring. As a result of the poor wiring work, the apartment catches on fire, and a tenant in one of the upstairs apartments is killed. Is Charlie guilty of a crime? If so, what crime and why? Write two or three sentences for your answer.

42

© 2005 Walch Publishing

Criminal Law

Crimes Against the Person: False Imprisonment

False imprisonment is the unlawful arrest or detention of another person without his or her consent. To be considered imprisonment, the victim does not have to be confined or placed in a cell. If the victim reasonably believes that he or she cannot leave or escape, then the victim is considered detained.

Darrell is driving Erik in his car. When Erik asks to be let out of the car, Darrell begins to drive very fast, making it impossible for Erik to get out of the vehicle. Has Erik been detained? Write two or three sentences for your answer.

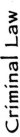

Daily Warm-Ups: Law

© 2005 Walch Publishing

Crimes Against the Person: Kidnapping

Kidnapping is the taking of another person without his or her consent, coupled with either movement of that person or hiding that person in a secret location. It is important to note that, under the law, a child is not considered capable of giving valid consent. Therefore, if the victim is a child, it does not matter if the child willingly went with the kidnapper.

Aggravated kidnapping, which is a more serious form of kidnapping, involves kidnapping for ransom (the kidnapper wants money for the return of the victim), kidnapping a child, or kidnapping with the intent to commit other crimes.

Terrence drives to a playground and asks Philip, an eight-year-old boy, to go for a ride with him. Philip gets in the car, and Terrence drives off with him. Has Terrence committed kidnapping or aggravated kidnapping? Write two or three sentences for your answer.

Daily Warm-Ups: Law

© 2005 Walch Publishing

Crimes Against the Person

Unscramble the letters to reveal the name of a crime against the person.

1. ALTUSSA _____

2. MDOCIIHE _____

3. AGNDPPIKIN _____

Daily Warm-Ups: Law

4. REMDUR _____

5. TRYBETA _____

© 2005 Walch Publishing

© 2005 Walch Publishing

46

Crimes Against Personal Property: Larceny

Larceny is the taking and carrying away of personal property belonging to someone else without that person's consent and with the intent to permanently deprive the owner of his or her interest in that property. Personal property that could be the subject of an act of larceny includes things such as cars, jewelry, collectibles, and anything else that has a physical form.

For the taking to be considered larceny, the property must have been in the possession of the owner at the time it was taken by the defendant. Also, the intent to permanently deprive the owner of his or her interest in the property must be present at the time that the property is taken.

Sheila wants to go out for the evening, but her car is being repaired. She knows that her neighbor keeps the keys in his car, so she decides to borrow it for the evening without his knowledge. Has she committed larceny? Why or why not? Write two or three sentences for your answer.

Crimes Against Personal Property: Embezzlement

Embezzlement is the fraudulent appropriation of personal property belonging to someone else by someone who has lawful possession of the property. It is different from larceny in that, with larceny, the owner must be in possession of the property at the time of the taking.

An embezzler has lawful possession of the property but does something with it that is inconsistent with the reason that he or she came into possession of the property.

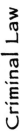

Daily Warm-Ups: Law

Carmen works at an upscale restaurant. Her job is to check coats. Rosa gives Carmen her $7,000 mink coat to check. Rosa's coat looks very similar to Carmen's $200 squirrel coat. When Rosa returns from dinner, Carmen gives her the squirrel coat and keeps the mink coat. Because it is late and Rosa is tired, she does not notice the difference and goes home with the wrong coat. Has Carmen committed larceny or embezzlement? Write two or three sentences for your answer.

© 2005 *Walch* Publishing

Crimes Against Personal Property: False Pretenses

False pretenses occurs when a criminal defendant deceives the owner of personal property into willingly giving up title to his or her property with intent to convert the property to personal use or profit. Persons who commit false pretenses do not have any lawful right to possession or any trust relationship. With false pretenses, the criminal defendant lies, and the victim relies upon that lie to the point that he or she is willing to give up title (the right of ownership) to his or her property. This is different from larceny, in which the owner is giving up just possession of his or her property.

If a criminal defendant tricks a victim into giving up title to his or her property, has he or she committed false pretenses or larceny? Write two or three sentences for your answer.

Daily Warm-Ups: Law

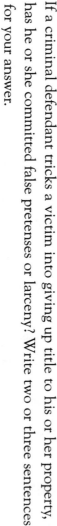

© 2005 Walch Publishing

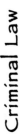

Criminal Law

Crimes Against Personal Property: Robbery

Robbery is the taking of the personal property of another from his or her possession by force (or the threat of immediate harm) with the intent to permanently deprive the owner of that property.

What is the difference between larceny and robbery? Write two or three sentences for your answer.

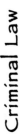

Daily Warm-Ups: Law

49

© 2005 *Walch* Publishing

Crimes Against Personal Property: Extortion

Extortion, which is sometimes referred to as blackmail, is the unlawful taking of property from another by threats of *future* harm. What is the difference between robbery and extortion? Time. In robbery, the threat of harm is immediate; in extortion, the threat of harm is in the future. It is important to note that the harm does not need to be physical harm. If you threaten to destroy someone's family by revealing a dreadful secret or to destroy his or her business, you have threatened harm sufficient for extortion.

Barry calls Marvin on the phone and says, "If you do not send me $1,000 in the mail, I am going to destroy your reputation in this community. I've got some great dirt on you, buddy. Make sure I get the cash by next Wednesday." In response to the call, Marvin mails Barry ten $100 bills. Has Barry committed extortion or robbery? Write two or three sentences for your answer.

© 2005 Walch Publishing

50

Criminal Law

Crimes Against Personal Property: Receiving Stolen Property

Receiving stolen property is the crime of receiving possession and control of stolen personal property known to have been obtained through crime with the intent to permanently deprive the owner of his or her interest in the property. Note that the property must be stolen. If someone receives property believing it to be stolen, but it actually has not been stolen, the person cannot be guilty of receiving stolen property. Further, a person can be convicted of receiving stolen property if he or she did not actually know that it was stolen but, based on the circumstances, should have known that it was stolen.

Percy owns a pawnshop, where people sell him used goods that he then resells at a higher price. One morning Keanu comes into Percy's shop and sells him a $5,000 ring for $100. Percy thinks that the ring must have been stolen, but he buys it anyway because it is such a great deal. It turns out that the ring was not stolen. Is Percy guilty of receiving stolen property? Write two or three sentences for your answer.

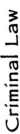

Daily Warm-Ups: Law

51

© 2005 Walch Publishing

© 2005 Walch Publishing

Crimes Against Personal Property: Forgery

Forgery is the creation or altering of a document so that it is false with the intent to defraud someone. Forgery also includes representing a forged document to be true when you know that it is false, even if the person making the representation is not the same person who forged the document. The most common example of forgery is when one person fakes the signature of another on a document of legal significance, such as a check or a contract.

Danny steals a check from his mother's checkbook, writes out a check to his friend Dawn, and signs his mother's name to the check in front of Dawn. Dawn then takes the check to the bank and deposits it into her account. Who is guilty of forgery? Write two or three sentences for your answer.

Daily Warm-Ups: Law

Crimes Against Personal Property: Malicious Mischief

Malicious mischief is the intentional destruction or damage of the personal property of another. To be malicious, the destruction or damage does not have to be the result of any particular feelings of hatred, resentment, or rage. It merely needs to be intentional.

Kevin is carrying Ahmet's radio, and they get into an argument. Kevin, who is normally very animated when he talks, is gesturing wildly with his hands and accidentally drops the radio. The radio shatters on impact. Should Kevin be arrested for malicious mischief? Write two or three sentences for your answer.

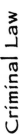

Daily Warm-Ups: Law

53

© 2005 Walch Publishing

Crimes Against Personal Property

Unscramble the letters to reveal the name of a crime against personal property.

1. YNCEALR _____

2. IRTOXETON _____

3. BRYREBO _____

4. GROYFER _____

5. LEMEZETEBMNZ _____

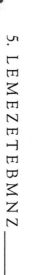

54

© 2005 Walch Publishing

Daily Warm-Ups: Law

© 2005 Walch Publishing

Crimes Against the Home or Dwelling: Burglary

Burglary is the entry of an occupied structure or a separately secured or occupied portion of the structure (home, garage, or shed) of another with the intent to commit a felony inside the structure. So, if a person walks into a home through a door that is left wide open with the intent to steal something from inside the home or to harm someone inside the home, that person has committed burglary. This is true even if he or she does not actually commit the felony once inside the home. It is important to note that the intent to commit the felony must be present at the time that the criminal defendant enters the structure.

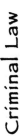

Daily Warm-Ups: Law

Raul is walking down Main Street and sees the front door of a beautiful Victorian mansion standing wide open. He has always wondered what the inside of a Victorian mansion looks like, and he decides to walk in just to take a look around. A couple of minutes after entering the mansion, he sees a guitar that is leaning against the wall. Raul grabs the guitar and runs out of the house. Has Raul committed burglary? Write two or three sentences for your answer.

Crimes Against the Home or Dwelling: Arson

Arson is the malicious burning or causing of an explosion for the purpose of damaging a structure belonging to someone else or damaging a structure for the purpose of collecting insurance proceeds for the loss. For the act to be malicious, it merely needs to be intentional or with reckless disregard for an obvious risk. If the purpose of the fire or explosion is to collect insurance proceeds for the damage, the structure does not have to belong to someone else.

Andy is staying at a friend's house. For amusement, he is foolishly throwing lit matches at a candle to see if he can get the candle to light. On one of his attempts, he misses the candle by several feet and hits a curtain, which promptly catches fire. The fire spreads through the house, and the home is destroyed. Has Andy committed arson? Write two or three sentences for your answer.

© 2005 Walch Publishing

Criminal Law

Crimes Against the Judicial System

Some acts are considered crimes against the judicial system. These crimes—perjury, subornation of perjury, and bribery—all involve activities that are designed to alter the outcome of judicial proceedings or official conduct.

Do you think it is important to punish people who perform activities that are designed to alter the outcome of judicial proceedings or official conduct? Why or why not? Write two or three sentences for your answer.

Daily Warm-Ups: Law

57

© 2005 Walch Publishing

Crimes Against the Judicial System: Perjury

Perjury is testifying falsely with respect to a material matter in a judicial proceeding. To be perjury, the false testimony must be intentionally false and not the result of a mistake or misperception of the facts. For a matter to be considered material, it must be of such a nature that it could affect the outcome of the proceeding.

Geri is a witness in the criminal trial of her boyfriend Jerry, who is being accused of murder. When asked what she was doing on the day of the crime, Geri states, "I was eating pizza from Antonio's with my parents. I hate Antonio's pizza." Everyone knows that Geri actually loves Antonio's pizza, and a hundred people would be willing to testify that she lied. Has Geri committed perjury? Why or why not? Write two or three sentences for your answer.

© 2005 Walch Publishing

Criminal Law

Crimes Against the Judicial System: Subornation of Perjury

A related crime to perjury is *subornation of perjury*, which is procuring or inducing someone to commit perjury. If a lawyer puts a witness on the stand knowing that the witness is going to commit perjury, the lawyer can be convicted of subornation of perjury. Also, if someone pays a witness to commit perjury, then that person has committed subornation of perjury.

Daily Warm-Ups: Law

Geri is a witness in a criminal trial. When asked what she was doing on the day of the crime, Geri answered, "I was eating pizza from Antonio's with my parents. I hate Antonio's pizza." Geri actually loves Antonio's pizza. It turns out that Silvio, a local restaurateur who is trying to drive Antonio's pizza place out of business, paid Geri $100 to lie because he knew there would be a lot of press coverage of the trial. Has Silvio committed subornation of perjury? Why or why not? Write two or three sentences for your answer.

59

© 2005 Walch Publishing

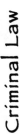

Crimes Against the Judicial System: Bribery

Bribery is offering or giving something of value to a public official for the purpose of influencing that official in the discharge of his or her duties. The thing of value that is offered or given is referred to as the bribe. Receiving or encouraging the offering or giving of a bribe is also considered bribery.

Randy is a building inspector. Donald owns a building that is being constructed by Jose. There are several problems with the building that are going to prevent it from being finished in time. If the building is not finished in time, Donald stands to lose quite a lot of money. Donald tells Jose to offer Randy $50,000 in exchange for Randy ignoring the problems with the building during his next inspection. Jose offers Randy the money, and Randy accepts it. Who in this scenario has committed bribery? Write two or three sentences for your answer.

© 2005 Walch Publishing

60

© 2005 Walch Publishing

Criminal Law

Parties to a Crime: Principals

Crimes are sometimes committed by more than just one person. Most of us have seen a movie in which a group of people decide to rob the local bank. Usually, there are about five people involved in planning the heist. Three people go into the bank for the robbery, one drives the getaway car, and one comes to his or her senses and backs out. Then family or friends who find out about the robbery afterward try to save their loved ones from the long arm of the law by hiding them in the basement or packing sandwiches for their flight to Mexico. In this scenario, there are several parties to the crime: principals, accomplices, and accessories after the fact. The *principal* is the person who actually engages in the act that constitutes the crime.

In the bank robbing example, how many acted as *principals*? Write two or three sentences for your answer.

Daily Warm-Ups: Law

© 2005 Walch Publishing

62

Parties to a Crime: Accomplices

An *accomplice* is a person who aids or encourages the principal to commit the offense. The accomplice for a crime could face a punishment that is as serious as the one the principal faces if the accomplice actually intended to aid or encourage the offense. If he or she did not, the accomplice's punishment would be less severe.

Three people go into the bank for the robbery, one drives the getaway car, and one comes to his or her senses and backs out. Then family or friends who find out about the robbery afterward try to save their loved ones from the long arm of the law by hiding them in the basement or packing sandwiches for their flight to Mexico.

In the bank robbing example, how many acted as accomplices? Write two or three sentences for your answer.

Criminal Law

Parties to a Crime: Withdrawal

Imagine that five people planned to rob a bank. One of the planners had a change of mind and backed out just before the heist. This person was still an accomplice to the crime because he or she helped commit the offense. This person could have avoided liability as an accomplice if he or she tried to inform the police or took some other action to prevent the crime. This is called *withdrawal*.

Imagine that the planner who backed out of the bank robbery before it was committed told the other perpetrators, "Look, I really think this is a bad idea. I'm backing out and you should, too." Do you think this should count as a withdrawal? Why or why not? Write two or three sentences for your answer.

Daily Warm-Ups: Law

© 2005 Walch Publishing

63

64

© 2005 Walch Publishing

Parties to a Crime: Accessory after the Fact

An *accessory after the fact* is someone who, knowing that a crime has been committed, assists the criminal in order to help him or her escape punishment. The punishment for an accessory after the fact is usually separate and less severe than that faced by the principal and any accomplices.

Imagine that five people robbed a bank together. After the robbery, several of the robbers told family members what they had done. The parents of one robber fixed up a hiding place for him in their attic. The boyfriend of another robber helped her leave the country so the police wouldn't catch her. The wife of a third robber was horrified. Although she didn't tell the police where her husband was, she refused to help him in any way.

Which of these family members acted as accessories after the fact? Write two or three sentences for your answer.

Daily Warm-Ups: Law

© 2005 Walch Publishing

Criminal Law

Inchoate Crimes: Attempt

Inchoate crimes are a group of offenses (attempts, solicitation, and conspiracy) that lead or are intended to lead to other crimes.

An *attempt* is an act done with the intent to commit a crime that falls short of completing the crime. To be guilty of an attempt, it must be shown that the criminal defendant did something beyond merely preparing to commit the crime. For example, if Ella is planning on burglarizing her neighbor's home and, in preparation, buys a pair of black gloves and a ski mask, she is not guilty of attempted burglary. If Ella goes to the house and tries—but fails—to get into the house, she is guilty of attempted burglary.

Daily Warm-Ups: Law

Bettina is so furious with her ex-husband that she decides to whack him in the head with a baseball bat the next time he comes to her house. She buys an aluminum bat, then goes to the batting cage and takes a few practice swings. Is Bettina guilty of an attempt? Write two or three sentences for your answer.

Inchoate Crimes: Conspiracy

A *conspiracy* is an agreement between two or more persons to commit a crime, coupled with an intent by at least two of the persons to see that the crime is committed. For a conspiracy to be present, at least two people must agree to commit a crime and at least two people must intend that the crime actually be committed. In addition, most states now require that there be some overt act in furtherance of the conspiracy. However, in contrast to an attempt, mere preparation is a sufficient act for a conspiracy.

Hank and Steve are coworkers. They get together in a hotel room and start planning the embezzlement of millions of dollars from the company. It turns out that Steve is serving as an informant for the police and is wearing a surveillance microphone. Is either Hank or Steve guilty of a conspiracy? Write two or three sentences for your answer.

Daily Warm-Ups: Law

© 2005 Walch Publishing

66

© 2005 Walch Publishing

67

Criminal Law

Inchoate Crimes: Solicitation

When someone urges, advises, asks, entices, or commands another person to commit a crime with the intent that the person actually commits the crime, he or she is guilty of *solicitation*. It does not matter if the person who is encouraged to commit the crime agrees to do so or if they actually commit the crime. Withdrawal—informing the police or taking some action to prevent the crime—is not a defense to solicitation.

Donna asks Martin to steal a car for her. She offers to pay him $500 if he steals one that is worth more than $10,000. A week later, she has a change of heart and calls him to say that the deal is off. Is she guilty of solicitation? Write two or three sentences for your answer.

Daily Warm-Ups: Law

Criminal Law: Defenses

Defenses to crimes come in two varieties: *mitigating defenses* and *exculpating defenses*.

Mitigating defenses are defenses that do not provide a basis for a finding of not guilty (otherwise referred to as an acquittal), but constitute a basis for making the penalty or punishment for the behavior less severe.

Exculpating defenses are defenses that provide the basis for an acquittal.

If you were on trial for a crime, would you rather have a good mitigating defense or a good exculpating defense? Write two or three sentences for your answer.

© 2005 Walch Publishing

68

Daily Warm-Ups: Law

Defenses: Criminal Capacity

To be convicted of a crime, a criminal defendant must have *criminal capacity*, meaning that he or she must have a fundamental ability to be accountable for his or her actions. The three defenses that are focused on the defendant's lack of capacity are the insanity defense, the defense of intoxication, and the infancy defense.

Do you think there should be a defense to criminal liability for children? What about for people who are insane? What about people who are intoxicated at the time of a crime? Why or why not? Write a paragraph to support your opinion.

Daily Warm-Ups: Law

© 2005 Walch Publishing

© 2005 Walch Publishing

70

The Insanity Defense

One of the more controversial capacity defenses is the *insanity defense*. Essentially, the defendant defends his or her action by saying that he or she was insane at the time. Courts in different jurisdictions rely on different insanity tests to determine whether the defendant's actions should be excused. The prevailing tests are the Durham (or New Hampshire) Test, the Irresistible Impulse Test, the M'Naghten Rule, and the Model Penal Code Test.

It is important to note that all defendants are presumed to be sane. Therefore, the burden of proof is on the defendant to demonstrate that he or she is insane.

Should the burden of proof for insanity be on the prosecutor or the defendant? In other words, should the prosecutor have to prove that the defendant was sane in all cases, or should the defendant have to prove that he or she was insane? Write two or three sentences to explain your opinion.

Daily Warm-Ups: Law

Insanity: The Durham Test

The *Durham Test*, which is also known as the New Hampshire Test, is the broadest of the insanity defenses. This means that it is the easiest one to prove. Under the Durham Test, a defendant is found not guilty if he or she can prove that he or she would not have committed the crime if it were not for the existence of his or her mental illness.

Sam suffers from a mental illness that makes him think that human beings are lunch meat. As a result, he walks around knocking random people to the ground and pouring ketchup and mustard on them. In his criminal battery trial, he proves that, if it were not for the existence of this mental illness, he would not have knocked these people to the ground. If the jurisdiction within which he is being tried uses the Durham Test, will Sam be convicted? Write two or three sentences for your answer.

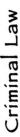

Daily Warm-Ups: Law

©2005 Walch Publishing

Insanity: The Irresistible Impulse Test

The *Irresistible Impulse Test* is slightly harder to prove than the Durham Test. Under this test, a defendant must prove that his or her mental illness created an impulse that he or she could not resist and that made it impossible to control his or her actions.

Alicia is fascinated with red things that have stems. As a result, every time she walks through the produce section of the grocery store, she sticks a bunch of apples in her pocket. She knows this is wrong, but she just cannot help herself. If the court trying Alicia for shoplifting follows the Irresistible Impulse Test, will Alicia be convicted? Write two or three sentences for your answer.

© 2005 Walch Publishing

Daily Warm-Ups: Law

Criminal Law

Insanity: The M'Naghten Rule

The *M'Naghten Rule* is harder to prove than the Irresistible Impulse Test. Under this test, a defendant must prove that, as a result of his or her mental illness, he or she did not understand the nature and quality of his or her act and did not know that his or her act was wrong.

Alicia is fascinated with red things that have stems. As a result, every time she walks through the produce section of the grocery store, she sticks a bunch of apples in her pocket. She knows this is wrong, but she just cannot help herself.

If the court trying Alicia for shoplifting follows the M'Naghten Rule, will Alicia be convicted? Write two or three sentences for your answer.

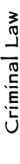

Daily Warm-Ups: Law

© 2005 Walch Publishing

73

Insanity: The Model Penal Code

The *Model Penal Code Test* is a combination of the Irresistible Impulse Test and the M'Naghten Rule. Under the Model Penal Code Test, the criminal defendant will avoid liability if he or she can demonstrate that he or she didn't know his or her conduct was wrong or that he or she could not control his or her conduct.

Alicia is fascinated with red things that have stems. As a result, every time she walks through the produce section of the grocery store, she sticks a bunch of apples in her pocket. She knows this is wrong, but she just cannot help herself.

If the court trying Alicia for shoplifting follows the Model Penal Code Test, will Alicia be convicted? Write two or three sentences for your answer.

Daily Warm-Ups: Law

© 2005 Walch Publishing

Criminal Law

Defenses: Intoxication

Intoxication is the disturbance of mental or physical capabilities that results from the use of drugs, alcohol, or medicine. If a criminal defendant becomes intoxicated voluntarily, he or she may only offer his or her intoxication as a defense if accused of a *specific intent crime* (burglary, assault, solicitation, attempts, conspiracy, larceny, robbery, forgery, embezzlement, and false pretenses) and then only if the intoxication prevented him or her from forming the intent required to commit the crime. If he or she became intoxicated just to establish the defense, then the defense will not be available.

Daily Warm-Ups: Law

Fredo begins drinking beer at noon; by early evening, he is very drunk. When the bartender tells Fredo that he cannot have any more beer, Fredo takes out his pocket knife and threatens to stab the bartender. Could Fredo possibly use intoxication as a defense? Write two or three sentences for your answer.

Defenses: Involuntary Intoxication

Intoxication is considered involuntary in any of three conditions. The first is if the defendant consumed an intoxicant because someone else forced him or her to. The second is if the intoxicant was prescribed by a doctor and the defendant did not know that it could have an intoxicating effect. The third is if the defendant did not know that he or she was consuming an intoxicant. Most jurisdictions treat the defense of involuntary intoxication as an insanity defense. The defense is judged according to the insanity test used by that jurisdiction.

Jamie is being treated for back pain and is given a powerful narcotic to dull the pain. The narcotic has an intoxicating effect of which Jamie was unaware before she consumed it. Was Jamie's intoxication voluntary or involuntary? If she commits a crime while intoxicated, how will most jurisdictions treat her intoxication? Write two or three sentences for your answer.

© 2005 Walch Publishing

Criminal Law

Defenses: Infancy

In most states, the *infancy* defense is available to children aged 14 or younger. Under the infancy defense, a child cannot be convicted of a crime. That is not to say, however, that the crime will go unpunished. Most states have juvenile justice systems that would try a child. If a crime is particularly serious, a court may rule that it is in society's best interests to try a child as if he or she were an adult.

State laws often require that the criminal record of children tried as juveniles to be *sealed*. This means that the convictions are treated as confidential information. Further, many states provide that once a child serves his or her juvenile sentence and becomes an adult, his or her juvenile record is *expunged*. This means that the record of the conviction is erased.

Jason is 10 years old when he breaks into a neighbor's home to steal a digital camera. Can he be convicted of the crime of burglary? If not, does this mean that he will not be punished? Write two or three sentences for your answer.

© 2005 Walch Publishing

Daily Warm-Ups: Law

Defenses: Justification Defenses

Among the exculpating defenses are a category of defenses referred to as *justification defenses*. Justification defenses are available when the circumstances of the crime dictate that, although the crime was committed, there was a justifiable excuse for the crime.

Justification defenses include self-defense, defense of others, defense of home, defense of other property, prevention of crime, and necessity.

Do you believe that there are occasionally situations in which someone would be justified in committing a crime? Write two or three sentences to explain your response.

Daily Warm-Ups: Law

78

Criminal Law

Defenses: Self-Defense

One defense in criminal cases is based on the idea of self-defense. This says that an individual may defend himself or herself against an imminent attack. The amount of force that is justifiable depends on the amount of force that appears likely to be used against the individual. For example, it is justifiable to use nondeadly force when it appears that nondeadly force or deadly force is going to be used against you. It is also justifiable to use deadly force when it appears that deadly force is going to be used against you. It is not justifiable to use deadly force when it appears that nondeadly force is going to be used against you.

© 2005 Walch Publishing

Daily Warm-Ups: Law

Jefferson is holding four loaves of bread. During an argument with Mary, Jefferson starts throwing the loaves of bread at her. To defend herself, Mary shoots Jefferson with a pistol and kills him. Can Mary claim that she acted in self-defense? Write two or three sentences for your answer.

Defenses: Defense of Others

An individual may also defend someone else against an imminent attack. The amount of force that is allowable is the same as under the defense of self-defense. For example, if you believed that your friend was in immediate danger of a deadly attack, you would be justified in killing your friend's potential assailant. Again, deadly force cannot be used to prevent a nondeadly attack.

Keisha tells Stella that she is going to knock Stella's teeth out if Stella does not give her $500 by next Thursday. Stella's friend, Shayla, hears the threat. She runs up to Keisha and punches her in the face. Will Shayla be acquitted of the charge of battery because she acted in Stella's defense? Write two or three sentences for your answer.

© 2005 Walch Publishing

Criminal Law

Defenses: Defense of Home

Nondeadly force can be used to prevent the unlawful entry of a home or an attack on the home, such as an act of vandalism. Deadly force can be used to prevent an attack, whether nondeadly or deadly, on an inhabitant of the home or to prevent the commission of a felony inside the home.

Melissa is asleep when she hears noises downstairs. She takes a pistol out of her nightstand and heads downstairs. As she reaches the bottom of the stairs, she sees a couple of men stealing her television and stereo. Melissa fires the pistol several times, hitting one of the men and killing him. Is her action justified?

Write two or three sentences for your answer.

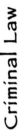

Daily Warm-Ups: Law

© 2005 Walch Publishing

Defenses: Defense of Other Property

Deadly force may never be used to defend property other than one's home. Nondeadly force can be used if it is necessary to defend an attack on property that is currently in one's possession.

Nondeadly force cannot be used if the attack could have been stopped by making a request for the perpetrator to stop or it is being used to regain possession of property that has already been taken, unless the force is used during a pursuit that began immediately after the taking.

Jorge is walking around with one of his favorite comedy CDs. Eli runs up to Jorge and takes the CD out of his hand. The next day, still furious about the incident, Jorge tracks Eli down, throws him to the ground, and takes the CD from Eli's pocket. Was Jorge's attack on Eli justified? Why or why not? Write two or three sentences for your answer.

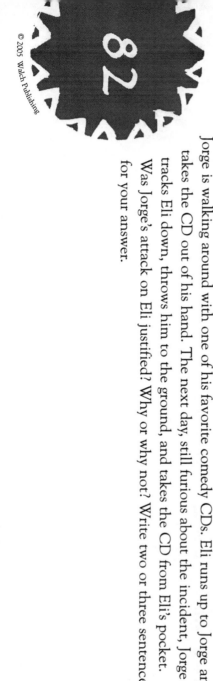

© 2005 Walch Publishing

Criminal Law

Defenses: Prevention of Crime

Nondeadly force may be used if it appears reasonably necessary to prevent a felony or a serious breach of the peace. Deadly force can only be used if it appears reasonably necessary to prevent a felony that involves a risk to human life.

Gregor finds out that Chris is establishing a number of offshore bank accounts. He recognizes this as a long-term plan on Chris's part to embezzle hundreds of thousands of dollars from the company for which they both work.

To stop the felony, Gregor walks into Chris's office and puts Chris in a choke hold. Is Gregor justified in the battery that he has committed against Chris? Write two or three sentences for your answer.

Daily Warm-Ups: Law

© 2005 Walch Publishing

83

Defenses: Necessity

Nondeadly force may be used if an individual reasonably believes that force is necessary to avoid a greater harm to him or to others. Deadly force may never be used to prevent harm to property.

It is also important to note that an individual cannot rely on the necessity defense if he or she caused the situation that led to the necessity.

Debbie starts a fire in her friend's apartment by intentionally kicking over a lit candle. As the fire starts to spread, she realizes that she has done something horrible.

Debbie grabs a very expensive Oriental rug and throws it on top of the flames to smother the fire. The rug is destroyed, and Debbie is arrested for malicious mischief. During her trial, Debbie asserts the defense of necessity and claims that she had to destroy the rug to prevent the fire from destroying the entire apartment building. Will the defense work? Write two or three sentences for your answer.

© 2005 Walch Publishing

84

Criminal Law

Defenses: Duress

If an individual commits a crime because that person reasonably believed that someone else would cause great bodily harm to him or her or to his or her family if he or she did not commit the crime, then the crime is excused. This *excuse of duress* cannot be used to excuse a homicide, however.

Bill holds a gun to Todd's head and orders Todd to drive him across the state line. Todd is drunk and knows that he should not be driving, but he does it anyway. When he is tried for driving under the influence, can he use the duress defense? What if, while driving Bill, Todd ran over and killed a pedestrian?

Write two or three sentences for your answer.

Daily Warm-Ups: Law

© 2005 Walch Publishing

85

© 2005 Walch Publishing

Criminal Law

Defenses: Mistake of Fact

For *specific intent crimes**, any mistake or ignorance of a fact that demonstrates that the defendant did not have the required mental state to commit the crime will excuse the crime. For all other crimes, only reasonable mistakes will excuse the crime.

*The inchoate crimes (solicitation, attempts, and conspiracy), crimes against personal property (larceny, robbery, forgery, embezzlement, and false pretenses), burglary, and assault.

Darius leaves work one night and picks up a coat that belongs to someone else. Darius's coat is bright red, and the coat that he took is dark blue, but Darius thought that he was grabbing his own coat. When he is tried for larceny, is the reasonableness of the mistake an issue? Write two or three sentences for your answer.

Daily Warm-Ups: Law

Criminal Law

Defenses: Mistake of Law

Ignorance of the law or a mistaken belief that one's actions are not criminal is generally not a defense to criminal behavior. If an individual has made a reasonable effort to understand or learn the law, however, a mistaken belief or ignorance of the law may excuse his or her criminal conduct. For example, if the law that the individual violates has yet to be published or if the individual was told by a police officer that the conduct was legal, then the crime would likely be excused.

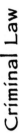

Daily Warm-Ups: Law

Laura is driving along a country road and has not been paying attention to the speed limit signs. She assumes based on the type of road and the fact that there are not a lot of homes around that the speed limit is probably very high. Therefore, she is driving at 60 miles per hour. A police officer pulls her over and informs her that the speed limit is actually 30 miles per hour. Laura says, "Oh, I'm sorry. I had no idea." Is this a valid defense to a reckless driving charge? Write two or three sentences for your answer.

© 2005 Walch Publishing

87

Defenses: Consent

The consent of the victim is only a defense to minor batteries and to crimes that require a lack of consent. Valid consent is required and is demonstrated when the consent is freely given by someone who has the capacity to consent. It is unlikely that a child, someone who is mentally ill, or someone who is intoxicated would be considered capable of giving consent.

Roger is at a soccer match and gets into an argument with Jim and Jim's ten-year-old son, Jimmy. The argument escalates and, simultaneously, the three of them start throwing punches. While Jimmy is biting Roger in the leg, Roger hits Jim in the face, then smacks Jimmy on the top of the head. In his criminal trial, Roger raises as a defense to his battery of Jim and Jimmy that they both consented because they freely engaged in the fight. Will this defense work with regard to the battery on Jim? What about the battery on Jimmy? Write two or three sentences for your answer.

© 2005 Walch Publishing

88

Criminal Law

Defenses: Entrapment

If a government official approaches a private citizen and initiates or encourages a crime, then the commission of the crime by the citizen is excused. Citizens cannot entrap other citizens, unless they are acting under the direction of the government. Also, if the citizen who commits the crime was predisposed to committing the crime, then the citizen cannot say he or she was entrapped. Whether a citizen is predisposed depends on the facts. For example, if the defendant had been arrested several times before for the same or a similar crime or if he or she expressed no hesitancy in agreeing to commit the crime, then it is likely that the court will find that he or she was predisposed to commit the crime.

Susana and Henry work together at a restaurant. Susana hatches a plan to embezzle money from the restaurant and approaches Henry to see if he is interested. It takes Susana months to convince Henry that he should participate in the crime. They are both eventually arrested. Henry claims that he was entrapped. Was he?

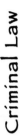

Daily Warm-Ups: Law

89

© 2005 Walch Publishing

Criminal Law: Review

Match the crime on the left with its definition on the right.

Crime

involuntary manslaughter

embezzlement

kidnapping

voluntary manslaughter

Definition

the fraudulent appropriation of personal property belonging to someone else by someone in lawful possession of the property

murder that has been provoked

the killing of another that results from "negligence" or from the commission of an unlawful act (other than a dangerous felony)

the taking of another person without his or her consent, coupled with either movement of that person or hiding that person in a secret location

© 2005 Walch Publishing

Criminal Procedure

Criminal Procedure

Criminal procedure is an area of the law that has to do with the rules that the police, prosecutors, courts, defense attorneys, and criminal defendants must obey when a criminal defendant is arrested and tried. Criminal procedure dictates what the police can and cannot do in investigating crime and governs how criminal trials are to be conducted.

Criminal procedure is essentially comprised of five stages:

1. police investigation

2. the pretrial process

3. the criminal trial

4. sentencing

5. appeals

Establishing and enforcing rules for criminal procedure is a balancing act between the power of the government and the rights of individuals. Many rights of U.S. citizens are found in the Bill of Rights. Name one aspect of the Bill of Rights that would affect criminal procedure.

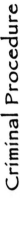

91

© 2005 Walch Publishing

Police Investigations

The police are responsible for investigating and solving crimes. The police must be very careful, when they are questioning potential suspects or searching for evidence, not to violate the suspect's constitutional rights. One of those constitutional rights is the Fourth Amendment right of people to be free from unreasonable searches and seizures. The general rule is that the police may not intrude into or search an area where a person has a reasonable expectation of privacy unless they have a properly issued and executed search warrant.

Name three places where you believe you should have a reasonable expectation of privacy. Why did you select those places? Should the police be allowed to search in those areas? Why or why not? Write two or three sentences for your answer.

Daily Warm-Ups: Law

© 2005 Walch Publishing

Criminal Procedure

Reasonable Expectation of Privacy

Whether a person has a reasonable expectation of privacy depends on the nature of the place searched and the location of the evidence that was seized. A person has a reasonable expectation of privacy in his or her home. Additionally, a person staying in another's home or in a hotel would likely have a reasonable expectation of privacy in the room in which he or she was staying, but probably not in the remainder of the building. There is no expectation of privacy in anything that could be seen by the public, such as garbage that is left outside for collection, the paint on the outside of a car, or land visible from an airplane or a helicopter.

Daily Warm-Ups: Law

The police suspect that Omar has committed a murder. They spot him walking through an airport and see blood stains on his luggage. They seize his luggage and collect the blood stains from it. Omar claims that the search is inappropriate because he has a reasonable expectation of privacy in his luggage. Is he correct? Write two or three sentences for your answer.

© 2005 Walch Publishing

Issuing Search Warrants

As a general rule, the police may not search an area where a person has a reasonable expectation of privacy unless they have a properly issued and executed search warrant. A warrant is properly issued if it meets all the following conditions:

- It is issued by a neutral, detached judge or magistrate (a judge or magistrate who has no interest in the criminal matter).

- It is supported by probable cause (there is a reasonable basis to believe that evidence will be found on the person or place searched).

- It specifically describes the place to be searched and the evidence to be seized. The judge or magistrate cannot rely on a police officer's conclusion that probable cause exists. It must be based on facts submitted by the police officer.

Jared is a judge in Jackson County. Jackson County recently started a compensation program that gives judges an extra $100 for every search warrant that they issue. If Jared issues a warrant, would it be properly issued? Write two or three sentences for your answer.

© 2005 Walch Publishing

Daily Warm-Ups: Law

Criminal Procedure

Executing Search Warrants

As a general rule, the police may not search an area where a person has a reasonable expectation of privacy unless they have a properly issued and executed search warrant. A warrant is properly executed if it meets all the following conditions:

1. It is executed by the police and not by a private citizen.

2. It is executed without unreasonable delay to make sure that the probable cause for issuing the warrant does not disappear.

3. It is executed after the police announce their purpose (unless an emergency exists).

Daily Warm-Ups: Law

4. The police search only the person or place specified (although they are allowed to seize evidence that is in plain sight).

Danica is suspected of committing armed robbery. The police are given a properly issued search warrant to search 14 Spring Avenue, which they believe is Danica's home. When they drive to Spring Avenue, they discover that Danica's car is parked outside 18 Spring Avenue. They execute the search warrant at 18 Spring Avenue and find valuable evidence. Was the warrant properly executed? Write two or three sentences for your answer.

Search Rule Exceptions

There are several exceptions to the general rule that the police may not intrude into or search an area where a person has a reasonable expectation of privacy unless they have a properly issued and executed search warrant. One exception is that the police may conduct a search without a warrant if it is conducted in connection with a lawful arrest. The police are allowed to search the area within the reach of the arrested person to make sure there are no weapons within reach. If the arrested person is in a car, this allows the police to search the passenger compartment. They may also search beyond that area if they think that other accomplices might be present.

Horace is arrested for aggravated battery. At the time of his arrest, Horace is seated in his car. In connection with the arrest, the police search the entire car. They find a knife under the passenger seat and a shotgun in the trunk. Can the knife and shotgun be introduced as evidence against Horace? Write two or three sentences for your answer.

© 2005 Walch Publishing

96

Criminal Procedure

Search Rule Exceptions: Vehicle Searches

Another exception to the general rule that the police may not intrude into or search an area where a person has a reasonable expectation of privacy unless they have a properly issued and executed search warrant is related to vehicle searches. If the police have probable cause to search any part of a vehicle, they may search the entire vehicle and any container within the vehicle that might contain the object for which they are searching.

Daily Warm-Ups: Law

Officer Schmidt has probable cause to believe that Victor's car contains a stolen antique chair. While searching the car, he sees a shoe box tucked under the front seat. He pulls out the shoe box from under the seat and opens it. Inside is a bag of heroin. Officer Schmidt seizes the heroin and arrests Victor. Was the seizure of the heroin legitimate? Write two or three sentences for your answer.

© 2005 Walch Publishing

97

Search Rule Exceptions: The Plain View Exception

The plain view exception is another exception to the general rule that the police may not intrude into or search an area where a person has a reasonable expectation of privacy unless they have a properly issued and executed search warrant. As the name implies, the police may seize evidence that is in plain view. For this exception to apply, all of the following factors must be present:

- The police officer had a right to be on the premises.

- The police discovered evidence of a crime that was in plain view.

- The police have probable cause to believe that what is seized is evidence of a crime.

The police have a warrant to search for stolen computers at Andrea's house. While conducting the search, they discover a pound of marijuana on Andrea's coffee table. Andrea's defense attorney objects to the use of the marijuana as evidence against Andrea because the warrant did not give the police authority to search for drugs. Was it appropriate for the police to seize this evidence? Write two or three sentences for your answer.

© 2005 Walch Publishing

Daily Warm-Ups: Law

Criminal Procedure

Search Rule Exceptions:
Valid Consent to Search

The police may also conduct a warrantless search if they receive valid consent to conduct the search. To be valid, the consent must be voluntary and must be given by someone who has the apparent authority to consent to a search of the particular location. For example, a parent can generally consent to a search of his or her child's room.

However, if the child's room is padlocked and the parents do not have a key, it is less likely that they can consent.

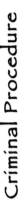

Daily Warm-Ups: Law

Officer Simpson thinks there is evidence of a crime in Jessica's house. While Jessica is out of town, Officer Simpson goes to her house and asks her gardener if it is all right to go inside and take a quick look around. The gardener lets him in. While inside, Officer Simpson finds the evidence he thought he would find. Is this search and seizure legitimate? Why or why not? Write two or three sentences for your answer.

99

© 2005 Walch Publishing

Search Rule Exceptions: Armed and Dangerous

The police may, without a warrant, conduct a limited search for weapons if they have a legitimate basis for stopping someone and they believe that the person is presently armed and dangerous. The police have a legitimate basis for stopping someone if they have a reasonable basis to believe that person is engaging in criminal activity. Once the police have stopped the suspect, they are allowed to conduct what is referred to as a protective search. If the police find weapons or contraband (something that is illegal to possess, such as drugs) during this protective search, it may be seized.

The police receive a tip that a jewelry store is about to be robbed. When they arrive at the scene to investigate, they see Wilma, a known armed robber who has recently been released from prison, walking toward the store with her hands shoved in her jacket pockets. Can the police stop Wilma and search her? Write two or three sentences for your answer.

© 2005 Walch Publishing

Daily Warm-Ups: Law

Criminal Procedure

Search Rule Exceptions: Pursuit of a Felon

The police may also conduct a warrantless search and seizure if they are in pursuit of a felon who is trying to escape. If the police are trying to apprehend a felon and that felon runs into his or her home, the police do not have to obtain a search warrant before they can enter the home. Notice that this exception is limited to felons (that is, people who are suspected of committing a serious crime).

Daily Warm-Ups: Law

Paulina is walking one of her purebred, well-groomed dogs. Although the town in which Paulina lives has a strict leash law that requires all dogs to be on a leash when outside, she believes that the leash messes up the dog's fur and refuses to leash the dog. Officer Hunter tries to stop Paulina and issue her a citation for violating the town's leash law. Paulina picks up her dog and runs into her home. Officer Hunter calls for backup, then runs into Paulina's home to apprehend her and seize her dog as evidence. Can he do this?

© 2005 Walch Publishing

© 2005 Walch Publishing

Criminal Procedure

Miranda Warning

If the police want to use a suspect's confession as evidence against him or her, they must be able to show that they gave the accused the following warning before interrogating the suspect:

> You have the right to remain silent. Anything you say can and will be used against you in court. You have the right to be represented by an attorney. If you cannot afford an attorney, one will be appointed for you.

This warning is called a Miranda warning because the content of the warning was dictated by the Supreme Court case *Miranda v. Arizona.*

Isabel is arrested and brought to the police station. She is placed in an interrogation room. When a detective enters the room, Isabel blurts out, "I did it. I committed the crime." At her trial, Isabel claims that her confession cannot be used against her because she was not given a Miranda warning before she confessed. Is she correct? Write two or three sentences for your answer.

Daily Warm-Ups: Law

Criminal Procedure

The Exclusionary Rule

If the police violate a suspect's constitutional rights to obtain evidence against the suspect, they are not allowed to use the evidence in the suspect's criminal trial. This is called the *exclusionary rule.*

What do you think is the purpose of the exclusionary rule? Do you think that evidence obtained in violation of a suspect's constitutional rights should be excluded from the trial? Why or why not? Write two or three sentences to explain your opinion.

Daily Warm-Ups: Law

© 2005 Walch Publishing

© 2005 Walch Publishing

Criminal Procedure

"Fruit of the Poisonous Tree"

In addition to losing evidence excluded by the exclusionary rule, the police may not be able to use any evidence obtained based on other evidence illegally obtained. This is referred to as the "fruit of the poisonous tree" doctrine. For example, if the police illegally seize a notebook from a murder suspect's house and that notebook contains the location of the murder weapon, the police will not be allowed to use the murder weapon as evidence. However, the weaker the link between what the police did wrong and the evidence that they eventually seized, the less likely that a court will prevent the evidence from being used. Therefore, if the police discover additional evidence based on further investigation or it appears that they would have found it eventually, the evidence will likely be admitted.

In the notebook example above, if the police had already obtained, but not executed, a valid warrant to search the place where the murder weapon was located, should they be allowed to admit the weapon as evidence? Write two or three sentences to explain your opinion.

Daily Warm-Ups: Law

Criminal Procedure

The Pretrial Process

After a felony suspect has been arrested, the government prosecutor must go through a number of procedural steps prior to taking the case to trial. First, there is an initial appearance. This hearing is held before a judge within one day of the arrest. At the initial appearance, the suspect is informed of the charges against him or her, bail is set, and, if necessary, an attorney is appointed to represent the accused. Next, the prosecutor must determine whether to officially charge the suspect and, if so, with what crime. It is within the prosecutor's discretion to charge a suspect, and he or she can dismiss the case for any reason at this stage. Typically, a prosecutor will dismiss a case if he or she does not feel that there is sufficient evidence to support a finding of guilt.

As you can see, the criminal prosecutor has a great deal of power and discretion in determining who is charged and prosecuted. Can you foresee any dangers or problems associated with allowing an individual so much power? Write two or three sentences for your answer.

105

© 2005 *Walch* Publishing

Preliminary Hearing and Probable Cause

After charges have been filed, the criminal defendant is entitled to a preliminary hearing. The purpose of the preliminary hearing is to determine whether there is probable cause to support the charges filed. This hearing is conducted much like a trial. If the judge finds that there is insufficient evidence to support the charge, the case is dismissed, and the suspect is released. However, if the police find additional evidence, the prosecutor may recharge the suspect at a later time.

If, after a preliminary hearing, a judge finds that there is insufficient evidence to support a criminal charge, should the government be allowed to continue to hold the suspect in custody for some period of time while they search for additional evidence? Write two or three sentences to explain your opinion.

© 2005 Walch Publishing

Daily Warm-Ups: Law

© 2005 Walch Publishing

Criminal Procedure

The Defendant Pleads . . .

If there is probable cause to support the charges filed against a criminal defendant, the case proceeds to arraignment. The defendant is asked to enter a plea (tell the court whether he or she is guilty or not guilty of the charges). A defendant can plead guilty, not guilty, or *nolo contendere*, which is Latin for "I will not contest it."

A *nolo contendere* plea means that the accused will accept punishment, but will not admit guilt. The legal significance of this plea is that a plea of *nolo contendere* cannot be used as evidence against the accused in a civil trial. If the defendant pleads guilty or *nolo contendere*, the case proceeds to sentencing. If the defendant pleads not guilty, the case proceeds to trial.

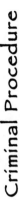

Daily Warm-Ups: Law

Kyle is on trial for aggravated battery. Kyle's victim, Adam, suffered serious injuries. Adam has filed a civil lawsuit against Kyle to recover the cost of his medical bills. Kyle is willing to accept criminal punishment for his action, but he wants to avoid having to pay Adam's medical bills. How should he plead? Write two or three sentences for your answer.

Plea Bargaining

It is quite common for the prosecutor and the defendant to agree on a mutually acceptable resolution of a case. This is called *plea bargaining*. How it typically works is that the defendant agrees to plead guilty, and the prosecutor either agrees to charge the defendant with a less serious crime or agrees to recommend a lesser punishment to the court. Plea bargains must be approved by the court.

What do you think of this practice? Are there any benefits? Can you foresee any unfortunate consequences of plea bargaining? Write two or three sentences to explain your opinion.

© 2005 Walch Publishing

Daily Warm-Ups: Law

Grand Jury

A grand jury indictment is a formal, written accusation of a crime setting forth the charges for which a criminal defendant will stand trial. Like trial juries, grand juries are comprised of ordinary citizens. There are important differences between grand juries and trial juries. For example, a criminal defendant cannot be forced to take the witness stand in front of the trial jury. A criminal defendant can be forced to appear before a grand jury (although he or she can refuse to actually say anything that would incriminate him or her). Unlike at a trial, the defendant does not have the right to be represented by an attorney in front of the grand jury.

Daily Warm-Ups: Law

Ling is ordered to appear before a grand jury. While Ling is on the stand, the prosecutor asks him a question. If Ling were to answer the question, he would have to admit that he has committed a crime. What should Ling say in response?

a. "I am asserting my First Amendment right to not incriminate myself."

b. "I am asserting my Fifth Amendment right against self-incrimination."

c. "Talk to the hand."

©2005 Walch Publishing

A Fair Trial

The United States Constitution provides for four basic rights for criminal defendants who stand trial. One of those rights is the right to a fair trial. To be considered fair, a trial must meet the following conditions:

- It must be held in public, so that the government cannot secretly arrest and charge people with crimes.

- It must be overseen by an impartial judge.

- It must be free from disrupting influences that could keep the jury from giving adequate consideration to the evidence.

- The defendant must be allowed to wear non-prison clothing during the trial.

Wyatt is charged with assaulting a neighbor. As it happens, the judge who heard Wyatt's case went to law school with the victim. After a trial, Wyatt is convicted. Did he receive a fair trial? Why or why not? Write two or three sentences for your answer.

Daily Warm-Ups: Law

© 2005 Walch Publishing

Criminal Procedure

Trial by Jury

One of the four Constitutional rights provided to criminal defendants who stand trial is the right to a trial by jury.

Defendants who are charged with serious offenses have a right to a trial by a jury of their peers. A crime that carries the potential of imprisonment for more than six months is considered a serious offense. Juries usually consist of 12 people, but can be as small as 6 people. The jury must be impartial and unbiased.

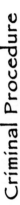

Daily Warm-Ups: Law

Rae is charged with reckless driving after being caught driving her car 100 miles per hour in a residential neighborhood. The maximum penalty that she faces if convicted of reckless driving is one year in prison. Because this is her first offense it is unlikely, but still possible, that she would get any prison time. Is Rae entitled to a trial by jury? Write two or three sentences for your answer.

© 2005 Walch Publishing

The Right to Effective Legal Representation

The United States Constitution provides criminal defendants with the right to be represented by an effective attorney. One of the most often used grounds for seeking a reversal of a conviction is that the defendant's attorney was ineffective. To show that his or her attorney was ineffective, the defendant must show that the attorney performed poorly and that, as a result of that poor performance, the defendant was wrongly convicted. This is not easy to demonstrate. Courts presume that the attorney was effective and tend to give deference to decisions and strategies that an attorney uses in the exercise of his or her professional judgment.

Robert is accused of committing a serious crime and is appointed an attorney to represent him. During the trial, the attorney falls asleep at the table on several occasions. As a result, he misses a number of opportunities to object to evidence that is improperly admitted against Robert. Robert is convicted and appeals the conviction. Should his conviction be upheld because he had counsel present? Write two or three sentences for your answer.

© 2005 Walch Publishing

Daily Warm-Ups: Law

Criminal Procedure

The Right to Confront Witnesses

The Sixth Amendment says that a criminal defendant has the right to confront witnesses against him or her. This is intended to give the accused the opportunity to question (or cross-examine) the witness in front of the jury. If the defendant has the opportunity to cross-examine a witness and chooses not to, the defendant's Sixth Amendment right is not violated. This is true even if the witness does not testify at the trial but testifies at an earlier hearing or proceeding and is unavailable to testify at trial.

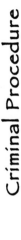

Daily Warm-Ups: Law

Byron is accused of stealing his friend's most cherished toy. The chief witness against Byron is Warren, who claims to have seen Byron take the toy. Warren testifies at the preliminary hearing; Byron's attorney elects not to cross-examine him. Before Byron's trial, Warren is killed. The court admits his preliminary hearing testimony. Because he is not present in the courtroom, he cannot be cross-examined. Does this violate Byron's Sixth Amendment rights? Write two or three sentences for your answer.

113

©2005 Walch Publishing

Daily Warm-Ups: Law

Tort Law

A *tort* is a legal wrong committed against someone's person or property. Torts fall into three general categories: intentional torts, negligent torts, and strict liability torts. In a tort case, someone has been injured or harmed in some way by someone else and is seeking to keep that person from causing further injury or harm to him or her and/or to recover financial damages as compensation for the injury or harm that he or she has suffered. When a victim brings a tort lawsuit, the victim is referred to as the *plaintiff*. Tort law focuses on compensating the plaintiff for harm or injury suffered. Contrast this with criminal law, which is focused mainly on punishing criminals for their behavior.

Daniel suffers a severe injury when he is punched by Elton. Use your knowledge of criminal and tort law to fill in the blanks in the following sentences.

In a tort case arising out of this incident, the primary focus would be to _____.

In a criminal case arising out of this incident, the primary focus would be to _____.

Tort Law

A Preponderance of the Evidence

Often, criminal behavior can also form the basis for a tort. It is possible that a criminal can be both prosecuted by the government for the crime and sued by his or her victim for the tort. In both the criminal case and the civil case, the person who committed the act would be referred to as the defendant.

In a criminal case, the defendant can only be found guilty if the prosecution proves its case "beyond a reasonable doubt." In civil cases, defendants are not found guilty or not guilty; they are found liable (or responsible) or not liable. In a civil case, the defendant can be found liable if the victim proves his or her case by a "preponderance of the evidence." This means that it is more likely than not that the defendant committed the act.

Which do you think is harder to prove, guilt beyond a reasonable doubt or liability by a preponderance of the evidence? Write two or three sentences for your answer.

©2005 Walch Publishing

© 2005 Walch Publishing

Intentional Torts

For a plaintiff in an intentional tort case to win, he or she must be able to show three things. First, he or she must show an act by the defendant. The act must involve a willful movement by the defendant. Second, the plaintiff must show that the defendant either intended to cause the consequence that resulted (referred to as specific intent) or that the defendant knew with substantial certainty that the consequences would result (referred to as general intent). Third, he or she must show that the consequence that resulted was caused by the defendant's act. For a tort case, the act is considered the cause if it was a substantial factor in bringing about the consequence.

Marcus is practicing kicking a football. His friend, Lucy, offers to help him by holding the ball. As Marcus approaches and starts to kick at the ball, Lucy removes the ball and Marcus ends up losing his balance and falling on the ground. Marcus's back is injured. Could he bring a tort lawsuit against Lucy? Write two or three sentences for your answer.

Intentional Torts: Battery

The tort of *battery* is a harmful or offensive touching of the plaintiff, which was intended by the defendant and resulted in injury or harm to the plaintiff.

A touching can be either direct (the defendant hits the plaintiff) or indirect (the defendant throws something that hits the plaintiff). The touching is considered harmful or offensive if it was not consented to by the plaintiff and it caused injury or, in the absence of an injury, a reasonable person would consider it offensive. Although a plaintiff may not have given express permission for a harmful or offensive touching, if he or she engaged in an activity in which such a touching is to be expected, then his or her consent will be considered implied.

Darren is playing goalie in a hockey game. Stavros shoots a puck at the net, and it hits Darren in the foot. Darren's toe is broken. Has Stavros committed a battery against Darren? Write two or three sentences for your answer.

117

© 2005 Walch Publishing

Intentional Torts: Assault

The tort of *assault* is an act by the defendant that creates a reasonable apprehension in the plaintiff that the plaintiff is about to suffer a battery.

A reasonable apprehension is found when the defendant has the apparent ability to carry out the battery. This does not mean that the plaintiff has to be afraid of the defendant. It merely means that the defendant has created an apprehension that he or she is going to commit the battery. Furthermore, if a defendant says that he or she is going to batter the plaintiff, but does not have the ability to commit the battery, there is no assault.

Sean is 6'4" and weighs 250 pounds. Jason is 5'6" and weighs 145 pounds. While on the beach one day, Jason walks up to Sean. He tells Sean that he doesn't like his attitude and that he is going to punch him in the stomach. Sean knows that he can defend himself, but he is pretty sure that Jason is going to hit him. Has Jason committed assault? Write two or three sentences for your answer.

© 2005 Walch Publishing

118

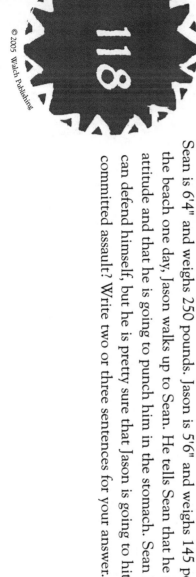

Daily Warm-Ups: Law

Intentional Torts: False Imprisonment

The tort of *false imprisonment* is the confinement or restraint of the plaintiff without his or her consent and without justification. For the tort of false imprisonment to be shown, the confinement or restraint does not have to come about as the result of physical force. A plaintiff can also be found to have been confined or restrained if the defendant threatened the plaintiff with physical force, put up barriers to prevent the plaintiff from moving, or threatened the plaintiff's property. However, to be considered confined or restrained, the plaintiff must not know of any reasonable means of escape.

Daily Warm-Ups: Law

Jamal, a store security guard, thinks that Dave might steal something because he is wearing baggy pants. Jamal grabs Dave by the arm and drags him into the security office, then tells him to wait there while he calls the police. Jamal leaves and locks the door to the security office. There is an air shaft over Dave's head. If he stands on the chair, he will be able to climb to safety. Can Jamal be held liable for false imprisonment? Write two or three sentences for your answer.

© 2005 Walch Publishing

119

© 2005 Walch Publishing

120

Intentional Torts: Emotional Distress

The tort of intentional *infliction of emotional distress* consists of an act that amounts to extreme and outrageous conduct and results in severe emotional distress. Extreme and outrageous conduct is conduct that transcends the bounds of human decency. To prove intentional infliction of emotional distress, the plaintiff needs to prove that the defendant acted recklessly with respect to the effect that his or her actions would have on the plaintiff. If the plaintiff is particularly susceptible to emotional distress and the defendant is aware of this when committing the extreme or outrageous act, the defendant's actions are considered reckless.

While La Shawna is sleeping, Heather places a spider in La Shawna's bed. When La Shawna wakes up, she sees the spider crawling on her arm. La Shawna is a big fan of spiders and is not startled at all. Heather is disappointed at La Shawna's reaction, and she lets it slip that she put the spider in the bed. La Shawna is bothered that Heather would try such a thing and sues her for intentional infliction of emotional distress. Will she win? Write two or three sentences for your answer.

Tort Law

Intentional Torts: Trespass

The civil wrong of trespassing is divided into two separate torts: trespass to land and trespass to chattels. A *trespass to land* is an intentional physical invasion of the plaintiff's real property (land and buildings). The physical invasion can be by the defendant or by an object that invades the plaintiff's real property as a result of the defendant's actions. A *trespass to chattels* is an intentional act that interferes with the plaintiff's right of possession in a chattel (any item of property that is not real property). The interference could be in the form of damages to the chattel or depriving the plaintiff of his or her right to possession of the chattel.

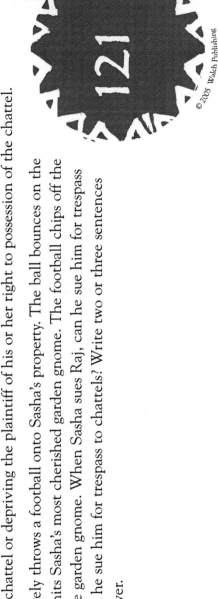

Daily Warm-Ups: Law

Raj deliberately throws a football onto Sasha's property. The ball bounces on the ground and hits Sasha's most cherished garden gnome. The football chips off the left ear of the garden gnome. When Sasha sues Raj, can he sue him for trespass to land? Can he sue him for trespass to chattels? Write two or three sentences for your answer.

© 2005 Walch Publishing

Intentional Torts: Conversion

The intentional tort of *conversion* is a trespass to chattels that is so serious that it warrants requiring the defendant to compensate the plaintiff for the full value of the chattel. For example, if Raj throws a football into Sasha's yard and the ball shatters Sasha's garden gnome (rather than just chipping it as in the previous activity), the tort of conversion has been committed.

Conversion can happen when the chattel is seriously damaged (as in the garden gnome example), stolen, or wrongfully detained. The longer the chattel is kept from its rightful owner and the more serious the damage, the more likely the act will be considered conversion instead of trespass to chattels.

Wendy takes Philip's bike without his permission and uses it for a couple of days. Is this trespass to chattels or conversion? What if she took it for an hour, but during that hour the bike was run over by a car and destroyed? Write two or three sentences for your answer.

© 2005 Walch Publishing

Defenses to Intentional Torts: Consent

Daily Warm-Ups: Law

If a plaintiff consents to the defendant's conduct, then the defendant cannot be liable for the intentional tort. There are two things that must be examined to determine whether the plaintiff truly consented. First, the plaintiff's consent must have been *valid*. This means that the consent was not given by mistake, under duress, or because of a misrepresentation from the defendant. Second, the act by the defendant must be within the bounds of the plaintiff's consent. For example, if the plaintiff and defendant willingly agree to play a basketball game together, but during the course of the game, the defendant intentionally trips the plaintiff and he or she is injured, then the defendant will be found liable. The intentional trip is not within the rules of the game and is not the type of activity to which the plaintiff consented.

A doctor tells a patient that the chances of suffering vision loss from a certain eye surgery are very slim. In fact, nearly half of those who undergo this surgery suffer vision loss. The patient consents to the surgery. Was this consent valid? Write two or three sentences for your answer.

Defenses to Intentional Torts: Self-Defense

When someone reasonably believes that he or she is being or is about to be attacked, that person may defend himself or herself. He or she may only use the amount of force that is reasonably necessary to protect against the attack, however. If someone knows that he or she is about to be hit by a spitball, that person cannot hit the spitballer with a baseball bat and claim the act was in self-defense. Self-defense is not available as a defense to a defendant who actually instigated (or caused) the events that led to the use of force. In other words, you cannot provoke someone into trying to take a punch at you and then hit the person and claim you were acting in self-defense.

Tammy and Winona are having an argument. Tammy takes a swing at Winona. To stop the punch from landing, Winona steps out of the way, grabs Tammy's arm, and flips her, seriously injuring Tammy's back. When Tammy sues Winona for battery, Winona claims self-defense. Who will prevail?

© 2005 Walch Publishing

Daily Warm-Ups: Law

Tort Law

Defenses to Intentional Torts: Defense of Others

The defense of *defense of others* is very similar to self-defense, except that instead of defending oneself, the defendant is acting to defend someone else. The amount of force that may be used is the amount of force that could have been used by the person who is being defended. With both self-defense and the defense of others, the attack that is being defended against must be happening or must be about to happen.

Daily Warm-Ups: Law

Tammy and Winona are arguing, and the disagreement turns violent. Dolly sees the argument. She watches as Tammy tries to punch Winona, and Winona flips Tammy onto her back. As Tammy is lying on the ground, Dolly runs over and jumps on Tammy, seriously injuring her legs. When Tammy sues Dolly for battery, Dolly claims that she was defending Winona from Tammy. Who will prevail? Write two or three sentences for your answer.

© 2005 Walch Publishing

Defenses to Intentional Torts: Necessity

Someone may interfere with or damage the property of another if it is reasonably necessary to prevent injury. However, the injury that is being protected against must be substantially worse than the interference or damage that is caused. *Public necessity* is an interference or damage that is done for the sake of the public good. *Private necessity* is an interference or a damage that is done for the sake of protecting the defendant's property. If someone successfully uses the defense of public necessity, he or she has no liability. If someone successfully uses the defense of private necessity, he or she is liable to the extent of the damage caused.

Quinton sees a boulder rolling down a hill toward a crowded playground. He quickly jumps into a parked truck and drives it in the path of the boulder. The boulder destroys the truck but is stopped in its tracks. The truck's owner sues Quinton for conversion. Quinton uses the defense of necessity. Was Quinton's necessity public or private? What will be the likely outcome of the lawsuit? Write two or three sentences for your answer.

© 2005 Walch Publishing

Tort Law

Defenses to Intentional Torts: Defense of Property

A person may use a reasonable amount of force to prevent a tort against his or her property. If it is possible to make a request for the *tortfeasor* (the person who commits the tort) to stop or to leave, however, that request must be made before force is used. Deadly force or force that causes serious injury may not be used unless the tort that is being committed might result in serious bodily injury.

Daily Warm-Ups: Law

Deborah sees Tran wander onto her property. It looks as if he doesn't realize that it is her property. However, Deborah is getting tired of people walking onto her property. Because she is fed up, she walks down to where Tran is standing and shoves him forcefully so that he is no longer on her property. When Tran sues Deborah for battery, she claims that she was acting in defense of her property. Who will prevail? Write two or three sentences for your answer.

Defenses to Intentional Torts: Discipline

Parents are allowed to use a reasonable amount of force to discipline their children. Whether the amount of force is considered reasonable depends on the circumstances.

Teachers stand *in loco parentis* (a Latin phrase meaning "in place of the parents"). This means that they are also allowed to use a reasonable amount of force to discipline their students. Courts tend to be more critical of a teacher's use of force than a parent's use of force.

Should parents be allowed to use physical force to discipline their children? Should teachers be allowed to use physical force to discipline their students? Write three or four sentences giving your opinion.

Daily Warm-Ups: Law

© 2005 Walch Publishing

Negligent Torts

Negligence is a particular kind of tort. For a plaintiff to demonstrate that a defendant has acted negligently, he or she must demonstrate all the following elements:

- The defendant owed the plaintiff a duty of care.
- The actions of the defendant violated or breached the duty of care.
- The plaintiff suffered damages.
- Those damages were caused by the defendant's action.

Daily Warm-Ups: Law

Give three examples of situations in which someone may owe a duty of care to someone else.

© 2005 Walch Publishing

© 2005 Walch Publishing

Duty of Care

To understand the general duty of care, you must understand the concept of the *foreseeable plaintiff*. For all human activity, a duty of care to act as a reasonable and prudent person is owed to any foreseeable plaintiff. Most courts consider anyone to be a foreseeable plaintiff if it could have been reasonably contemplated that he or she would be injured by the defendant's conduct. This is called the "zone of danger" test. The remaining courts interpret the foreseeable plaintiff much more broadly and essentially consider everyone a foreseeable plaintiff.

Freddie is playing in a professional basketball game. A fan in the crowd has been harassing Freddie for most of the game, and Freddie eventually loses control of his temper. He picks up a chair and throws it at the fan who has been harassing him. The chair misses that fan and hits another fan, causing a broken arm. Using the "zone of danger" test, is the fan who was hit by the chair a foreseeable plaintiff? Write two or three sentences for your answer.

Daily Warm-Ups: Law

Professional Duty of Care

The general duty of care extends to ordinary people in the conduct of their lives. More specific duties of care apply to certain people. A professional (a person with special skill or training in a particular field, such as a doctor, a lawyer, an accountant, or a pilot) is held to a higher duty of care. A professional must exercise his or her special judgment, skill, and knowledge. In addition, this person must possess and exercise the skill and knowledge that a member of his or her profession in good standing in the community would possess and exercise.

James is a Certified Public Accountant who works for a large corporation. Every spring he supplements his income by doing tax returns on the side for individuals. This spring he has been very busy at work and has not had time to read all of the new tax regulations. As a result, he ends up claiming deductions for a number of his clients for items that are no longer allowed by the IRS. One of his clients is audited by the IRS and has to pay a large penalty. This client sues James for negligence. Who will prevail? Write two or three sentences for your answer.

Daily Warm-Ups: Law

131

© 2005 Walch Publishing

Vehicular Duty of Care

The duty owed by an automobile driver to his or her passengers depends on whether the passenger is paying for the ride. If the passenger is not paying for the ride, the driver is required to let the passenger know about nonobvious defects in the vehicle and to exercise reasonable care in the operation of the vehicle. If the passenger is paying for the ride, the driver is also required to make reasonable inspections of the vehicle to determine dangerous conditions.

Acme Insurance Company employs 2000 people at its New York headquarters.

Many of these people live in remote suburbs and have to drive a long distance to get to work. As an employee perk, Acme Insurance Company decides to start operating a van pool. Employees who want to use the van pool must pay a small fee of $1 per day for the service. Is Acme Insurance Company required to make reasonable inspections of their vans to determine dangerous conditions? Write two or three sentences for your answer.

© 2005 Walch Publishing

Daily Warm-Ups: Law

Tort Law

Landowner's Duty of Care 1

The duty of care required of someone who owns or occupies land depends on where the harm occurs. A landowner or an occupier must exercise reasonable care with respect to his or her behavior or the behavior of others on his or her property to protect those outside of the property from an unreasonable risk of harm. For example, a landowner would be liable if he or she allows guests to fire bottle rockets at passing automobiles and someone is injured as a result.

Daily Warm-Ups: Law

Heidi owns a home in the city. One day while she is at work, a neighbor's son runs onto her property, hides behind some bushes on the property, and starts throwing rocks at homes across the street. The neighbor's son ends up breaking a number of windows. Should Heidi be held responsible for this? Why or why not? Write two or three sentences for your answer.

© 2005 Walch Publishing

Tort Law

Landowner's Duty of Care 2

If harm occurs on someone's property, the duty of care required of the landowner depends on who is harmed. People who are harmed on someone else's property are divided into three categories: invitees, licensees, and trespassers. An *invitee* is someone who enters the land in response to an invitation by the landowner or occupier. This does not include people who are social guests. Invitees include people who visit a museum or a store, provided they are there for a purpose that the landowner or occupier reasonably intends. With respect to invitees, a landowner or an occupier must warn invitees of dangerous conditions, make reasonable inspections to discover dangerous conditions and correct them, and exercise reasonable care with respect to the operations of the property.

As stated above, invitees include people who visit a museum, as long as they are there for a purpose that the property owner reasonably intends. Would a salesperson who comes to a museum to try to sell glass display cases be considered an invitee? Write two or three sentences for your answer.

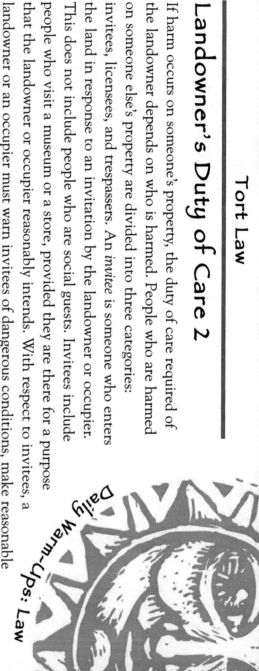

© 2005 Walch Publishing

134

Tort Law

Licensees and Trespassers

A *licensee* is someone who enters another's land with permission for his or her own benefit. A social guest is considered a licensee. With respect to licensees, a landowner or an occupier must both warn licensees of dangerous conditions and exercise reasonable care with respect to the operations of the property.

A *trespasser* is someone who enters the land without permission and without justification. If a landowner or an occupier does not know about the trespasser, he or she owes the trespasser no duty of care. If he or she learns of the trespasser's presence, he or she must warn the trespasser of nonobvious and highly dangerous conditions and exercise reasonable care with respect to the operations of the property.

Orlando has a pool at his house and has told Art that he can use the pool whenever he wants. Orlando is watching television one night when Art arrives and goes for a swim. Orlando has no idea that Art is there. Is Art a licensee or a trespasser? Write two or three sentences for your answer.

135

© 2005 Walch Publishing

Negligence Per Se

When the defendant's conduct does not rise to the level required by the applicable duty of care, the defendant has breached the duty of care. If the defendant's conduct is against the law, then it is impossible for the defendant to argue that he or she has met his or her duty of care. This is referred to as *negligence per se*.

Wesley is a passenger in a car that is being driven by Rebecca. Rebecca is driving 75 miles per hour on a wet road that normally has a speed limit of 25 miles per hour. She loses control of the car and slams into a tree, seriously injuring Wesley. Will Rebecca be able to argue that she met her duty of care (to exercise reasonable care in the operation of the vehicle)? Write two or three sentences for your answer.

© 2005 Walch Publishing

136

Speaks for Itself

In a few cases, the mere fact that something happened may establish a breach of duty. This is referred to as *res ipsa loquitur*, which is a Latin phrase meaning "the thing speaks for itself." To establish *res ipsa loquitur*, the plaintiff must demonstrate three things: that the event that led to the damages is not the sort of thing that happens unless someone was negligent, that the thing that caused the damage was in the defendant's sole custody, and that the plaintiff was not at fault.

Trevor is walking down the street when he is knocked unconscious by a bowling ball. He later learns that Malik owns and operates a bowling ball manufacturing company on the second floor of the building that Trevor was walking past when he was hit by the bowling ball. Will Trevor be able to show that Malik breached a duty of care? If so, under what theory? Write two or three sentences for your answer.

Daily Warm-Ups: Law

© 2005 *Walch* Publishing

137

© 2005 Walch Publishing

Demonstrating Damage

Damage is the third element required to demonstrate a case of negligence. A plaintiff can recover damages for personal injury, including the cost of medical treatment, the amount of lost income, an amount that is reasonable to compensate the plaintiff for pain and suffering, and the amount of lost future earning potential. A plaintiff may also recover the cost of repair for damaged property or, if the property was destroyed, the fair market value of the property. If the defendant's actions were particularly offensive, reckless, or malicious, the plaintiff may also be able to recover punitive damages. These additional damages are intended to punish the defendant for his or her behavior.

Kirby is riding his bicycle when he is struck by a car driven by Alison. At the time of the accident, Alison is under the influence of alcohol. Will Kirby be able to recover punitive damages against Alison? Write two or three sentences for your answer.

Daily Warm-Ups: Law

Causation

The fourth and final element required to demonstrate negligence is *causation*. For causation to be shown, the plaintiff must show that the defendant's act was both the actual cause and the legal cause of the harm suffered by the plaintiff. To determine whether the defendant's conduct was the *actual cause* of the plaintiff's damages, courts generally apply a "but for" test. If the harm to the plaintiff would not have occurred "but for" the act of the defendant, the defendant's act will be considered the actual cause. However, when there are several factors that contributed to the harm to the plaintiff, the "but for" test is insufficient. In these cases, the plaintiff must show that the defendant's act was a substantial factor in causing the plaintiff's injury.

Susan throws a rock at George, who is standing in a crowd of people. Dorothy and Chandler are two of the people standing in the crowd. When the rock is thrown, Dorothy tries to jump out of the way and hits Chandler in the mouth, causing injury to his teeth.

Was Susan's act the actual cause of Chandler's injury? Write two or three sentences for your answer.

139

© 2005 *Walch* Publishing

Tort Law

Proximate Cause

To be the *legal cause* of harm (also known as the *proximate cause*), the resulting harm must have been foreseeable and not the result of a crime or intentional tort committed by a third party. Basically, if a defendant's acts sets a chain of events in motion that results in a harm that is reasonably to be expected, the defendant's act will be considered the actual cause. It is quite possible that something that is the actual cause will not be the legal cause.

Susan throws a rock at George, who is standing in a crowd of people. Dorothy and Chandler are two of the people standing in the crowd. When the rock is thrown, Dorothy tries to jump out of the way and hits Chandler in the mouth, causing injury to his teeth.

Was Susan's act the legal (or proximate) cause of Chandler's injury? Write two or three sentences for your answer.

Contributory and Comparative Negligence

A defendant who is accused of acting negligently may claim that the plaintiff was also negligent. In some states, if the plaintiff was also negligent and his or her negligence contributed to his or her injuries, he or she cannot recover any damages from the defendant. These states are applying a *contributory negligence rule*. In other states, the court will assign a percentage of fault to the plaintiff's negligence and will reduce the amount of damages available to the plaintiff by that amount. For example, if the plaintiff suffered $100 in damages, but his or her negligence was responsible for 30 percent of those damages, he or she will be awarded $70 from the defendant. These states are applying a *comparative negligence rule*.

Ashley suffers $100,000 in damages when she and Fatima collide while riding their bicycles. The court in which the suit is filed follows the contributory negligence rule. If Ashley is 50 percent responsible for her damages, how much will she be awarded?

141

© 2005 *Walch* Publishing

Daily Warm-Ups: Law

Tort Law

Strict Liability Torts

Strict liability stands for the concept that in certain situations a defendant is liable for a plaintiff's damages without any requirement that the plaintiff prove that the defendant was negligent. To demonstrate that a defendant is liable for a strict liability tort, a plaintiff must show the existence of the following elements:

- That the defendant had an absolute duty to make something safe

- That the defendant breached that duty

- That the plaintiff suffered damages

- That the defendant's breach was the actual and legal cause of those damages

People who own wild animals can be held strictly liable for damages that are caused by those wild animals unless the plaintiff did something to bring about the injury. In some states, dog owners can also be held strictly liable if their dog bites someone. However, in many states, dog owners would only be held liable if they knew that their dog had a tendency to bite.

Do you think dog owners should be held strictly liable if their dog bites someone? Write two or three sentences to explain your opinion.

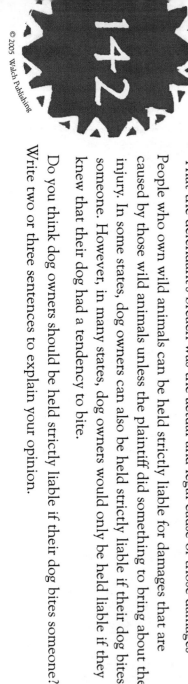

© 2005 Walch Publishing

Areas of the Law: Intellectual Property

The drafters of the U.S. Constitution wanted to protect the rights of individuals engaged in creative works. Therefore, they included the following clause in Article I, Section 8 of the U.S. Constitution:

Congress shall have the power . . . to promote the Progress of Science and useful Arts, by securing for limited Times to Authors and Inventors the exclusive Right to their respective Writings and Discoveries.

Intellectual Property is an area of the law that is devoted to the protection of the rights of people who create or invent. Intellectual Property law is broken into four principal subject matters: copyright, trademarks and service marks, patents, and trade secrets.

Why do you think the drafters of the U.S. Constitution wanted to ensure that creators and inventors would have exclusive rights in the things that they created or invented? Write two or three sentences for your answer.

Daily Warm-Ups: Law

143

© 2005 Walch Publishing

Copyright

A copyright protects certain rights of authors of original literary, dramatic, musical, or artistic works. Copyright protection is established and defined by federal law.

The following expressions of creativity can be protected by a copyright: a literary work, a dramatic work, a musical work, a pantomime or choreographic work (such as a dance arrangement), a picture, a graphic work, a sculpture, a motion picture, a sound recording, and an architectural work.

For the following scenarios, decide whether Rob can get copyright protection. Write *yes* or *no* on the line after each scenario.

1. Rob has written a song. _____

2. Rob has copied down the words to a song written by someone else. _____

Daily Warm-Ups: Law

144

© 2005 Walch Publishing

© 2005 Walch Publishing

Intellectual Property Law

Tangible Form

To be copyrightable, a work must be fixed in a tangible form of expression. This means that it must be written down or recorded. A poem or song lyric that you make up and say to your friends is not copyrightable, unless you have recorded it or written it down.

Copyright protection does not extend to ideas, but rather to how an idea is expressed. For example, while you can copyright a movie script, you cannot copyright a general plot for a movie. This is probably why so many movies seem the same.

Daily Warm-Ups: Law

While at a national monument, Jonathan decides that he is going to pretend to be a tour guide. He steps up in front of a large group of tourists and proceeds to make up a hilarious story about the monument. Does he have copyright protection for his story? Why or why not? Write two or three sentences for your answer.

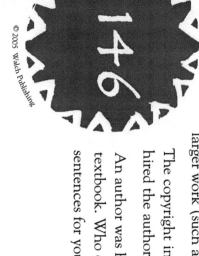

© 2005 Walch Publishing

146

Intellectual Property Law

Work Made for Hire

Once a work is fixed in a tangible form of expression, what does the author have to do to secure copyright protection? Nothing. That's right. Nothing. The copyright in the work immediately becomes the property of the author, unless it is a "work made for hire" or the author has agreed to give his or her rights to someone else.

A work is considered a "work made for hire" if the author agrees that it is to be considered a work made for hire; it is a work prepared by an employee within the scope of the employee's job (meaning, essentially, that it is work that the employee was hired to do); or it is a work specially ordered for use within a larger work (such as a soundtrack recording for a motion picture).

The copyright in a "work made for hire" belongs to the person or company that hired the author.

An author was hired by Walch Publishing for the express purpose of writing a textbook. Who owns the copyright in the textbook? Why? Write two or three sentences for your answer.

© 2005 Walch Publishing

Intellectual Property Law

Rights of the Copyright Owner

Under United States copyright law, the owner of a copyright is the only person who can reproduce or make copies of the work, create an adaptation or some other work that is based on the copyrighted work, distribute copies of the work, publicly perform or display the work, and perform sound recordings of the work. The copyright owner is also the only person who can authorize others to do any of these things.

A rock band, Anger for the Establishment, is upset because a web site has placed its latest album on-line and is allowing users to download the album for free.

Daily Warm-Ups: Law

Anger has a copyright for the album. Is the web site violating Anger's copyright? Write two or three sentences for your answer.

© 2005 Walch Publishing

Copyright Infringement

A violation of a copyright owner's exclusive rights is called an *infringement* of the copyright. Not every use of a copyrighted work is considered an infringement, however. Copyright law allows for "fair use" of copyrighted works. In determining whether the use of a copyrighted work is "fair," a court looks at four factors. One factor is the purpose and character of the use, including whether such use is of a commercial nature or is for nonprofit educational purposes. If the use is commercial in nature (the user is trying to profit from the use), it is less likely that the use will be considered "fair." Another factor is the nature of the copyrighted work. The more original or creative the copyrighted work is, the less likely that the use will be considered "fair." Works that are factual in nature, rather than fictional, are generally given less protection.

Sanjay has a copyright for a photograph that he took. Geoff decides to put that photograph on a series of postcards and sell them for profit. Is it more likely or less likely that a court would consider Geoff's use of Sanjay's work "fair"? Write two or three sentences for your answer.

Intellectual Property Law

Determining Fair Use

A court looks at four factors to determine whether a use is "fair." The first two are the purpose and character of the use, and the nature of the work. The third factor is the amount and substantiality of the portion used in relation to the copyrighted work as a whole. The more of a work that is used, the less likely that the use will be considered "fair." The fourth factor that a court would examine is the effect of the use upon the potential market for or value of the copyrighted work. The more that the use negatively impacts the value or potential market for the copyrighted work, the less likely that the use will be considered "fair."

Daily Warm-Ups: Law

An actor has written a 300-page autobiography that reveals a number of secrets about his life and career. Before the book is published, a magazine prints a 20-page excerpt from the book. The excerpt reveals several of the secrets presented in the book. As a result, the book's publisher decides that it probably will not sell as many copies as originally hoped and cancels the contract with the actor. Is it more likely or less likely that a court would consider the magazine's use "fair"? Write two or three sentences for your answer.

Copyright Notice

A copyright notice alerts the world that the author is claiming copyright protection for his or her work. However, a copyright notice is not required by law and is not required for the author to get copyright protection. The use of a copyright notice can be helpful in the event that someone else tries to claim a copyright for the same work, because it is harder for that person to demonstrate that he or she did not know that the work was previously copyrighted. A copyright notice consists of either the copyright symbol © or the word *copyright*, the year that the work was first published, and the name of the owner of the copyright. If Arthur Author published a book in 1995, his copyright notice would look like this:

© 1995 Arthur Author—or—Copyright 1995 Arthur Author

Find the copyright notice for a textbook. When was the book published? Who is the owner of the copyright?

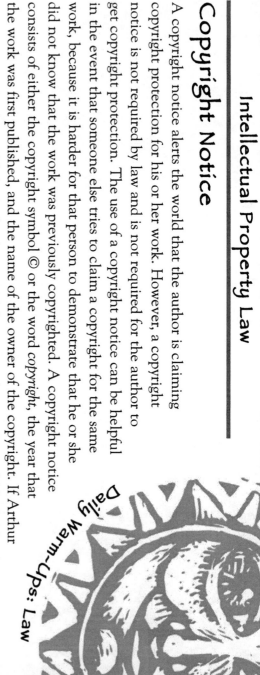

Daily Warm-Ups: Law

150

© 2005 Walch Publishing

Intellectual Property Law

Copyright Registration

Another means of ensuring copyright protection is to register it with the U.S. Copyright Office. Again, this is not required. However, there are some advantages to registering your copyright. One advantage is that it creates a public record of the copyright. Another is that registering the copyright makes it possible to file an infringement suit against someone whom you believe is violating your copyright.

Registration is very easy. It requires the mailing of two copies of the work to the Copyright Office along with a completed application form and a filing fee.

Daily Warm-Ups: Law

Jordi thinks that Ty is violating his copyright. Jordi has had the copyright for 10 years but has never registered it with the Copyright Office. Can Jordi sue Ty for infringement? Write two or three sentences for your answer.

© 2005 Walch Publishing

Length of Copyright Protection

How long does copyright protection last? For a work that is fixed in a tangible form on or after January 1, 1978, the copyright protection begins at the moment that the work is fixed in a tangible form and ends 70 years after the author's death. If there is more than one author of the work, copyright protection ends 70 years after the last surviving author's death. If the work was a "work made for hire" or the author is unknown, copyright protection ends 95 years after the work was published or 120 years after the work was fixed in a tangible form, whichever is shorter.

For works that were fixed in a tangible form and published or registered before January 1, 1978, copyright protection did not begin until the work was published or until it was registered (if registered in unpublished form). Copyright protection for these works lasted for 28 years, but that term could be renewed for an additional 28 years.

Tanya writes a play on January 1, 2005. She dies on January 1, 2050. When did her copyright start and when does it end?

© 2005 Walch Publishing

152

Daily Warm-Ups: Law

Intellectual Property Law

Trademarks and Service Marks

A *trademark* is a word, phrase, symbol, or design that identifies and distinguishes the source of an individual's or a company's products from those of others. Examples of familiar trademarks are the shape of the Coca-Cola bottle, the Nike swoosh, the Energizer Bunny, and the term *Pentium*, which is a registered trademark of Intel Corporation.

A *service mark* is similar to a trademark except that it identifies and distinguishes services instead of products. HBO and Cinemax are examples of service marks, both of which are owned by Time Warner Entertainment Company.

Itzahk starts a company that makes video games and decides to call it "High Flying Video Games." He creates a company logo that features a winged video game flying over a city skyline. Can Itzahk trademark the logo?

Daily Warm-Ups: Law

153

© 2005 *Walch* Publishing

Eligibility for Trademark Protection

To be eligible for trademark or service mark protection, the mark must be used in commerce. This means that, for a trademark, the mark must be placed on the goods, the container that holds the goods, or the displays that advertise the goods, and the goods need to be sold or transported. For a service mark, the mark must be used or advertised in the sale or display of the services. The mark does not, however, have to be used in commerce before it is claimed. Rather, a mark can be claimed based on the intent to use the mark in commerce. The United States Patent and Trademark Office will not register the mark until it has been used in commerce.

Nancy, an unemployed high school student, has come up with a catch phrase for herself: "I'm a little sister with big attitude." She hopes that if she uses it around her classmates, they will think she is really cool and she will become more popular. To keep anyone else from using the phrase, she tries to register it as a trademark with the United States Patent and Trademark Office. Will the phrase be registered? Write two or three sentences for your answer.

© 2005 Walch Publishing

Trademark Infringement

If the owner of a registered trademark files a lawsuit against someone else claiming infringement of the mark, the court will find infringement if there is a "substantial likelihood of confusion" between the registered trademark and the infringing mark. There does not have to be actual confusion between the marks, merely the possibility that a substantial number of purchasers would be misled or confused as to the source of the different products or, in the case of a service mark, different services.

Panda Toys holds a registered trademark for their company logo, a cuddly Panda named Petey that carries a blanket. A company named Panda Pencils also has a panda on its logo. This panda, named Perry, carries a pad of paper and a pencil. Panda Toys files a suit against Panda Pencils, claiming that their logo infringes on the Petey the Panda mark. Panda Toys has not introduced any evidence to show that anyone has actually been confused by the two marks. Could they still prevail in the infringement lawsuit? Write two or three sentences for your answer.

© 2005 Walch Publishing

Patents

A *patent* is a grant given to an inventor for his or her invention. The patent gives the inventor the right to exclude others from making, using, or selling the invention. There are three types of patents, all of which are issued by the United States Patent and Trademark Office. They are

- *utility patents*, for an inventor who invents or discovers any new and useful process or product or an improvement of an existing process or product. An example of a process would be a way of operating a computer. An example of a product would be the computer itself.

- *design patents* for an inventor who invents a new, original, and ornamental design of a product. The design patent covers only the appearance of the product.

- *plant patents* for an inventor who invents or discovers and reproduces any distinct and new variety of plants.

Jared has invented a new plant holder that has a unique and artistic shape. If he were to seek a patent for this invention, for what type of patent should he apply? Write two or three sentences for your answer.

156

© 2005 Walch Publishing

Daily Warm-Ups: Law

Intellectual Property Law

Patents for New Products or Processes

To be granted a utility patent, the process or product must be new and useful. To be considered useful, the invention must have a useful purpose and must operate in such a fashion that it fulfills that useful purpose. In other words, if you design an engine that is supposed to convert cheese into fuel for your car, but when it is actually operated, it merely burns the cheese beyond recognition, it will not be considered useful.

Patents are not given for ideas; they are given for actual products or processes.

Daily Warm-Ups: Law

You are the owner of a chain of fast-food restaurants. Describe a new and useful product or process for a restaurant for which you may be able to secure a utility patent. Feel free to supplement your description with a drawing. Write two or three sentences for your answer.

© 2005 Walch Publishing

© 2005 Walch Publishing

Patents for Improvements

Utility patents are also given to new and useful improvements to existing products or processes. In addition to requiring that the improvement is new and useful, the United States Patent and Trademark Office will also look to see if the improvement is "obvious." A patent will only be granted for an improvement that is sufficiently different from the prior invention that it would not be obvious to someone who works on a regular basis with the product or process.

Jeremiah has a patent for a machine that turns churned butter into a cream-colored latex paint. His neighbor, Keiko, realizes that, by adding different colored dyes to the churned butter, the resulting latex paint color can be changed. Keiko applies for a utility patent for this improvement to Jeremiah's machine. Will she be granted a patent? Write two or three sentences for your answer.

Daily Warm-Ups: Law

© 2005 Walch Publishing

Intellectual Property Law

Who Can File for a Patent?

In most cases, patent applications can be made only by the inventor. There are several exceptions to this rule. For example, if the inventor has died or is legally insane, a legal representative for the inventor may file. Also, if an inventor assigns or transfers his or her right in the invention to a third party, that third party may apply for the patent. Further, if the inventor refuses to apply for a patent, anyone with an ownership interest in the invention (including a coinventor) may apply for the patent.

Employees of the United States Patent and Trademark Office are not allowed to apply for a patent, nor are they allowed to acquire an interest or a right in a patent, unless that interest or right was acquired through an inheritance.

While employed by Vicki's Products for Children, Gavin invents a new toy. After Gavin leaves the company, Vicki's Products for Children wants to apply for a patent on his invention. What must the company do before it can apply for the patent? Write two or three sentences for your answer.

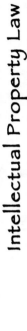

Daily Warm-Ups: Law

© 2005 Walch Publishing

Intellectual Property Law

Patent Rights

A patent gives the inventor the right to exclude others from making, using, or selling the invention. It does not give the inventor the right to make, use, or sell the invention. This is a very important distinction. The inventor must still abide by all laws governing the use of the product or process that he or she has invented.

Fredericka invents a new type of automatic weapon and receives a patent for her invention. She then attempts to sell the weapon in New York, where automatic weapons are banned. When she is prosecuted in New York for violating the automatic weapon ban, she claims that her patent right allows her to sell the weapon anywhere in the United States. Is she correct?

Intellectual Property Law

Patent Infringements

If an inventor finds that someone else is making, using, or selling his or her invention, he or she can file an infringement lawsuit to stop the other person. He or she could seek compensation for the other party's infringement on his or her patent rights. If someone wishes to make, use, or sell another's invention, but wants to do so in a manner that does not violate the inventor's patent rights, he or she can seek to obtain a license from the inventor. The license is a contract under which (typically) the inventor would receive payment in exchange for a promise not to sue the party who wishes to make, use, or sell the invention.

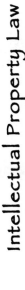

Roald discovers that Henry is using Roald's invention without his permission. Roald has known Henry for years and does not really want to sue Henry for infringement. Roald did, however, invest a lot of time, money, and energy into his invention. He thinks that it is reasonable for him to be compensated for Henry's use. What could Roald do in this situation? Write two or three sentences for your answer.

Patent Number

A product that is patented must be marked with the word *Patent* and the number of the patent that is assigned by the United States Patent and Trademark Office. If a patented product is not so marked, the inventor cannot recover damages for infringement of the patent unless he or she notified the infringer of the infringement and the infringer continued to infringe after the notice.

You may have seen products that are marked with the phrase *Patent Pending.* This phrase means that a patent has been applied for, but it has no legal effect. The inventor does not get any rights under the law by merely applying for a patent.

Hector has invented a new filter for a vacuum cleaner that automatically cleans itself. Because one of the selling points of the filter is how clean and fresh it looks, he chooses not to clutter it with the word *Patent* and the patent number assigned when his patent was granted. After his patent is granted, he learns that Sven has developed a vacuum filter that infringes on his patent, and Hector sues Sven for damages. Will he get them? Write two or three sentences for your answer.

© 2005 Walch Publishing

Trade Secrets

A *trade secret* is information that gives a person or a company a competitive advantage over its competitors who do not know the information. Examples of trade secrets include, for example, a list of customers, the recipe for a restaurant's "secret sauce," or a way of manufacturing a product. To get trade secret status, the person or company that has the information a secret. If someone believes that his or her trade secret keep the information a secret. If someone believes that his or her trade secret has been misappropriated (taken unlawfully) by someone else, he or she can file a lawsuit to stop that party from using the trade secret. He or she can receive compensation in the form of damages for the use.

A company that makes fish sticks has invented a new recipe. The recipe makes fish sticks with such a delicious taste and texture that the company is bound to have a big market advantage over its competitors. The company's president is so excited about it that he goes on a televised cooking show, discusses the recipe, and demonstrates how the new recipe is used. Does the company have a trade secret in this recipe? Write two or three sentences for your answer.

© 2005 Walch Publishing

164

Bankruptcy Law

The U.S. Constitution authorizes Congress to create uniform bankruptcy laws. The first such law was passed in 1800. Since then, U.S. bankruptcy law has evolved a great deal. The most recent changes to bankruptcy law were signed into law in April of 2005.

Here are two terms related to bankruptcy law:

- A *creditor* is a person or company that is owed money by a person or company that is seeking bankruptcy protection.

- A *debtor* is a person or company that is seeking bankruptcy protection.

The primary purposes of U.S. bankruptcy law are to give an honest debtor the ability to get relief from overwhelming debt, and to ensure that creditors are repaid in a logical and orderly manner to the extent that the debtor has the ability to repay the debt.

Only the federal government has the authority to create bankruptcy laws. States are not allowed to create their own bankruptcy law. Why does or why does it not make sense for there to be only one uniform bankruptcy law in the United States? Write two or three sentences to explain your opinion.

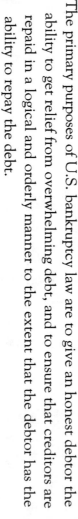

Bankruptcy Law

Bankruptcy Law

Bankruptcy Discharge

Bankruptcy law's purpose of giving an honest debtor the ability to get relief from overwhelming debt is accomplished through *discharge*. A discharge releases a debtor from personal liability for specific debts. This means that the debtor is not required to repay the debts. It also serves as a permanent injunction against creditors, stopping them from collecting a discharged debt. Creditors that violate the discharge could be cited for contempt by the bankruptcy court and be forced to pay a fine.

Certain types of debts cannot be discharged, including debts for child support or alimony, debts owed to the government for penalties or fines, and debts owed for personal injury caused as a result of operating a motor vehicle while intoxicated.

Fernando files for bankruptcy protection and is granted a discharge. After the discharge, he stops making his child support payments. Fernando claims that his responsibility for paying child support was discharged along with the rest of his debts. Were they? Write two or three sentences for your answer.

© 2005 *Walch Publishing*

© 2005 Walch Publishing

Types of Bankruptcies

The U.S. Bankruptcy Code provides for five types of bankruptcies. Each type is referred to by the number of the code chapter that covers that type. One type is Chapter 7 bankruptcy (also known as a liquidation or "straight" bankruptcy). Another type is Chapter 11 bankruptcy (also known as a reorganization bankruptcy). There is also Chapter 13 bankruptcy, the adjustment of debts of individuals with regular income, and Chapter 12, the adjustment of debts of a family farmer with regular annual income. Another type is Chapter 9 bankruptcy. This kind of bankruptcy gives a municipality—such as a city, a town, a county, or a school district—a period of relief from its creditors. During this period of relief, the municipality comes up with a plan to adjust its debts. The adjustment can result in the lowering of the debts, the elimination of some debt, or the extension of time within which a debt must be repaid. This adjustment is referred to as *debt reorganization*.

The City of Anytown is having trouble paying its debts and decides to file for bankruptcy protection. Which type of bankruptcy would the city file? Why? Write two or three sentences for your answer.

Bankruptcy Law

Chapter 7 or Liquidation Bankruptcy

In a Chapter 7 case, most debts are cancelled in exchange for a surrender of some of the debtor's property. When the debtor files for Chapter 7 bankruptcy, a *bankruptcy trustee* is appointed to manage the bankruptcy. The Chapter 7 debtor gives the trustee a great deal of information about the debtor's property, income, and debts. It is the trustee's job to see that the creditors are paid as much as possible.

According to the new bankruptcy law signed in April 2005, a debtor who goes through a Chapter 7 bankruptcy cannot file another Chapter 7 case for eight years from the date that the original Chapter 7 bankruptcy petition was filed.

Daily Warm-Ups: Law

Walter files for a Chapter 7 bankruptcy on March 1, 2006. A trustee is appointed, and the case results in a discharge of most of Walter's debts on March 1, 2007. Several years later, Walter is again in a financial bind, and he decides to file for another Chapter 7 bankruptcy on February 1, 2015. Is this allowed? Write two or three sentences for your answer.

© 2005 Walch Publishing

© 2005 Walch Publishing

168

Chapter 11, or Reorganization Bankruptcy

A Chapter 11 bankruptcy is very similar to a Chapter 9 bankruptcy, except that it is normally used by corporations or partnerships (although it can be used by individuals) instead of municipalities.

In a Chapter 11 case, the debtor's goal is to have the court approve a plan of reorganization under which some of its debts are discharged and others are restructured to be less burdensome. While a trustee is appointed to manage a Chapter 7 case, this only happens in a handful of Chapter 11 cases. When a debtor files for a Chapter 11 bankruptcy, the debtor becomes a separate entity, known as the *debtor in possession*, or DIP. A DIP performs many of the tasks in a Chapter 11 case that a trustee would perform in a Chapter 7 case. The DIP controls the debtor's assets, examines claims to property made by the creditors, and files detailed reports that are required by the court. The debtor remains the DIP until the plan of reorganization is approved by the court.

Name at least two differences between a Chapter 7 bankruptcy and a Chapter 11 bankruptcy.

Daily Warm-Ups: Law

Family Law

Family Law

Family law is an area of the law that focuses on family relationships. Family law involves topics such as marriage, divorce, child custody, and child support. Family law is principally a matter of state law, meaning that laws related to the family are generally created by state legislatures. Marriage, however, has significant meaning in federal law because a great number of federal laws look at marital status to determine federal rights and obligations. A prime example is federal tax law, which contains 179 separate provisions in which marital status plays some role in determining the rights or requirements for individual taxpayers. Another example is federal laws relating to employment. These laws include allowing employees to take time off from work to care for their marital partner and providing for continuation of health insurance for marital partners after an employee dies.

Should marital status play a role in determining things such as tax benefits or health benefits? Why or why not? Write two or three sentences to explain your opinion.

Daily Warm-Ups: Law

Marriage

Marriage is a voluntary, government-recognized agreement between two people to be united as a couple for life. Each state makes laws that define what constitutes a legal marriage. These laws include specific requirements that usually include the following:

- a marriage license issued by the county clerk or clerk of the court

- that the participants are over the age of 18 or have the consent of a parent

- requirements about who may legally perform the wedding ceremony

- whether the marriage certificate needs to be signed by witnesses of the ceremony

Marriages performed in another state, or even another country, are usually considered valid throughout the United States, as long as the marriage was valid where it was performed.

Joan is 16 years old and lives in Alabama. Alabama law requires that marriage participants be over the age of 18. In order to get married, Joan lies about her age. She then moves to Wisconsin. Will Wisconsin legally recognize her marriage? Write two or three sentences for your answer.

© 2005 Walch Publishing

© 2005 Walch Publishing

Family Law

Common Law Marriage

Fifteen states and the District of Columbia recognize what is known as *common law marriage*, which is a marriage that is created without a license and a ceremony. The requirements for what constitutes a common law marriage vary from state to state, but, generally speaking, the couple must do the following: they must live together for a significant period of time, they must represent to others that they are a married couple (by doing things like sharing a last name or referring to each other as husband and wife), and they must intend to be married. Because marriage is an agreement between two people, both parties must want to be married.

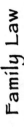

Daily Warm-Ups: Law

Octavio and Paula have lived together in the District of Columbia for 15 years. They refer to each other in public as husband and wife. In addition, Paula had her last name legally changed to be the same as Octavio's. Although he intends to stay with Paula forever, Octavio never wants to get married. Will the District of Columbia recognize this as a common law marriage? Write two or three sentences for your answer.

Divorce

States create laws to determine how and when a marriage is terminated. *Divorce* is the termination of a marriage by an order of the court. Each state creates its own laws about what constitutes valid reasons for seeking a divorce. These reasons are referred to as *grounds for divorce*. In almost every state, all that is required for there to be adequate grounds for divorce is for one spouse to want a divorce and to be certain that the marriage cannot be saved. If this is the case, the parties are said to have *irreconcilable differences*. States that recognize irreconcilable differences as a ground for divorce are referred to as *no-fault divorce jurisdictions*.

Ginger and Rex live in a no-fault divorce jurisdiction. Their marriage has been troubled for several years and, eventually, Ginger decides that she no longer wants to be married. She believes that there is no chance that she and Rex can repair the marriage. Will Ginger be able to get divorced from Rex? Why or why not?

Daily Warm-Ups: Law

© 2005 Walch Publishing

Prenuptial Agreements

© 2005 Walch Publishing

In a divorce proceeding, the married couple must decide how to divide the things that they own. This includes everything from the house, the cars, and the money in their bank accounts to their dishes, books, and compact discs. They must also agree on how to divide the debts that they owe. This could include the home mortgage, the car payments, and unpaid student loans. If the couple are unable to agree, the court will decide how their property and debts are to be divided.

Involving the court in this process is time consuming and expensive. Most couples try to come to an acceptable agreement themselves.

Daily Warm-Ups: Law

Some couples choose to decide how their property will be divided in a divorce before they get married. These agreements are referred to as *prenuptial agreements*.

Write one argument in support of having a prenuptial agreement in place. Then write one argument against having a prenuptial agreement in place.

© 2005 Walch Publishing

Child Custody

One of the most difficult aspects of a divorce is determining child custody. If the couple has children, they must decide how they are going to raise and care for those children. Child custody involves both physical custody and legal custody.

Having *physical custody* of a child means that the parent is responsible for supervising activities in the child's daily life. This includes making sure that the child gets to school, is fed adequately, and has a safe place to sleep. *Sole physical custody* is when one parent has exclusive responsibility for the child's daily life. If one parent has sole physical custody, the other parent will typically be given visitation rights, which refers to that parent's ability to occasionally spend time with the child. *Joint physical custody* is when the parents share, as equally as possible, the responsibilities for the child's daily life.

Write one argument in favor of sole physical custody. Then write one argument in favor of joint physical custody.

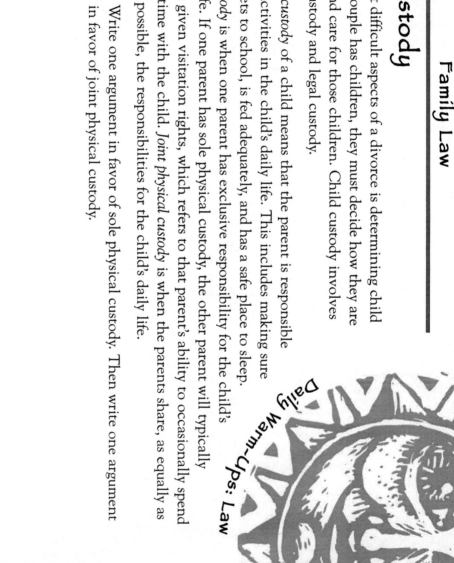

Daily Warm-Ups: Law

© 2005 Walch Publishing

Family Law

Legal Custody

Legal custody is the responsibility for making important decisions about a child's life and future. This includes decisions about appropriate medical treatment, where the child will be educated, and what religious faith, if any, the child will practice.

As with physical custody, a court can give one parent sole legal custody or order the parents to share joint legal custody. Even when one parent is given sole physical custody of a child, a court may still order that the parents share joint legal custody.

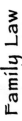

Daily Warm-Ups: Law

If a court orders joint physical custody, it is unlikely that it will order sole legal custody. Why do you think this is the case? Write two or three sentences for your answer.

Child Support

In addition to deciding who will have custody of a child, decisions must also be made about how to provide financially for the child. If one parent has sole physical custody, the other parent (referred to as the noncustodial parent) will likely have to pay child support to the custodial parent. This money is intended to cover the expenses necessary to raise the child. It is not meant to compensate (pay) the custodial parent for his or her efforts in raising the child.

If the parents share joint physical custody, the parent with the higher income may be required to pay child support to the other parent. Child support obligations are typically ordered by the court. Parents who fail to make required child support payments may be held in contempt of court. This means that the parent will have a certain period of time to make the missed payments. If the payments are not made, the court can then put the defaulting parent in jail. It can also garnish (take) wages.

Do you think a judge should be allowed to put someone in jail for refusing to make child support payments? Why or why not? Write two or three sentences to explain your opinion.

© 2005 Walch Publishing

© 2005 Walch Publishing

Becoming a Lawyer

Becoming a Lawyer: Education

If you think you might want to practice law, you should know what becoming a lawyer involves. A lawyer must first graduate from high school (or take a high school equivalency exam), graduate from college with a four-year (bachelor's) degree, and then graduate from law school. Full-time law school students usually graduate in three years. Many students attend law school on a part-time basis, however, and graduate in four years or more. Certain practice areas, such as patent law, require more schooling beyond law school.

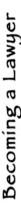

Daily Warm-Ups: Law

College students who want to attend law school can choose from a wide variety of majors to prepare for their future careers. Which of the following areas of study do you think would be most helpful in preparing for a career in law: communications, business, criminology, chemistry, or psychology? Why? Write two or three sentences to explain your opinion.

Becoming a Lawyer: Testing

In addition to attending approximately seven years of school beyond high school, those interested in becoming a lawyer must also prepare to take a great many tests during their school years and beyond.

During the application process for law schools, prospective law students must take the Law School Aptitude Test, or LSAT. The LSAT is about three hours and thirty minutes long and consists of six sections that test analytical reasoning, logical reasoning, and reading comprehension. The test requires a writing sample, and it includes an experimental section of analytical reasoning, logical reasoning, or reading comprehension. The results of the LSAT are crucial to getting into law school. Because a large number of law school applicants are not coming directly from college, work experience is looked at very critically. LSAT, grade point average, and work experience are weighed equally.

How many sections are there to the LSAT? In which section of the LSAT would this question have been?

Daily Warm-Ups: Law

© 2005 Walch Publishing

178

Becoming a Lawyer: Testing

Exams in most law school courses are several hours long. They are designed to judge the student's ability to spot legal issues and demonstrate sound legal analysis. Because of the intensity of study, the time commitment required to succeed, and the cost of tuition, approximately one out of every eight students who start law school quits.

Law school graduates who wish to practice law must take the bar exam for the state or states within which they want to practice. The bar exam consists of two separate exams: the multistate exam (multiple choice) and the state law exam (essay). Each exam takes approximately seven hours; therefore, it takes two days to take the entire bar exam. The multistate exam covers areas of the law that are fairly uniform throughout all 50 states. The state exam covers areas that are unique to the state within which the candidate intends to practice law.

Why do you think there are so many tests for lawyers? Write two or three sentences to explain your opinion.

Daily Warm-Ups: Law

179

© 2005 Walch Publishing

Becoming a Lawyer: Career Choices

Many law school graduates either never practice law or switch to careers that do not involve practicing law. Examples of law school graduates who went on to pursue other careers include Bill Clinton and Abraham Lincoln (former presidents of the United States), Steve Young (former quarterback for the San Francisco 49ers and broadcaster), Scott Turow and John Grisham (bestselling authors), and Francis Scott Key (composer of *The Star-Spangled Banner*). The study of law is much more than just training for being a lawyer. It allows students to develop their analytical thinking and logical reasoning. Law students devote many hours to the study of the United States Constitution and to the legislative process. This helps them understand the mechanics of government and can be helpful in the pursuit of government careers.

Name a career in which a legal education may be helpful. Explain why you think a legal education would be helpful in this career. Write two or three sentences for your answer.

© 2005 Walch Publishing

Daily Warm-Ups: Law

Teacher's Guide

1. Answers will vary, but should show an apprecia-
   tion for the necessity of law in establishing and
   maintaining order in society.

2. John Adams was emphasizing that the United
   States should be governed by the rule of law and
   that the law should apply equally to all men.

3. With the states maintaining power over trade and
   defense, there was very little political stability
   in the United States. Foreign countries were
   unwilling to enter into agreements with the
   United States, because the individual states did
   not have to abide by those agreements. In matters
   of finance, the states each established their own
   monetary and taxation systems, which created
   economic instability between the states.

4. Allowing amendments ensures that the U.S.
   Constitution addresses changes in the political,
   social, and economic climate of the nation. As
   examples, the Thirteenth Amendment (1865)
   abolished slavery, the Fifteenth Amendment

(1870) allowed newly freed black slaves the right
to vote, and the Nineteenth Amendment (1920)
guaranteed women the right to vote.

5. Answers will vary, but should be supported by a
   reasoned explanation.

6. The First Amendment sets forth the freedoms of
   religion, speech, and peaceable assembly. Students'
   opinions will vary, but should be supported by a
   reasoned explanation.

7. Answers will vary, but should be supported by a
   reasoned explanation.

8. Quartering is allowed in a time of war, but only in
   accordance with the law.

9. No. This is exactly the type of behavior that the
   drafters of the U.S. Constitution were trying to
   prevent.

10. Yes. While it does not prevent the government
    from taking private property, it does require the
    government to provide "just compensation" for
    the property that is taken.

Daily Warm-Ups: Law

Teacher's Guide

11. There is no Sixth Amendment right to counsel until a criminal prosecution has begun. Under *Miranda*, the right to counsel begins prior to being questioned by police.

12. Answers will vary, but should be supported by a reasoned explanation. Essentially, the Founding Fathers believed that there was less likelihood that a tyrannical act of the government would be upheld by a jury of citizens than if the case were decided by a single judge.

13. Answers will vary, but should be supported by a reasoned explanation.

14. The Ninth Amendment is intended to make it clear that the Bill of Rights is not to be considered a comprehensive and exhaustive list of the rights of American citizens.

15. Answers will vary, but should be supported by a reasoned explanation. Essentially, the drafters wanted to be careful to not create a central government that was overly powerful.

16. Students should do this activity after completing Activities 6–15.

Fourth—the right to be protected against unreasonable searches and seizures

First—freedom of religion

Eighth—the right to be protected against excessive bail

Fifth—the right to due process of law

17. This is prohibited by the U.S. Constitution. The power to declare war is reserved for the federal government under Article 1, Section 8.

18. Answers will vary, but should be supported by reasoned analysis. Examples of laws that may be different from state to state include speed limits; requirements for getting a marriage, driver's, or business license; and what constitutes criminal activity.

19. Answers will vary. Typically, local ordinances address such issues as waste collection, public parks, zoning, building codes, and sanitation.

Teacher's Guide

20. Students should do this activity after completing Activities 17–19.

the power to make laws—legislative

the power to declare law unconstitutional or invalid—judicial

the power to appoint judges and certain governmental officials—executive

21. This makes sense in accordance with the principle of proportional representation for the House of Representatives. Students' opinions about the number of representatives there should be may vary.

22. No. The president does not have line-item veto power and must approve or reject the bill in its entirety or do nothing with the bill.

23. The clerk did not take Bernie's filing because bankruptcy cases can only be filed in the United States Bankruptcy Courts.

24. Judicial review is the ability to review and reverse the decisions and actions of the other branches of government. It acts as a check against the legislative and executive branches because it could invalidate an action that they have taken that is contrary to prevailing law.

25. The president is vested with the power to appoint justices, and those appointments often reflect the political tendencies of the president and his party. Republican presidents tend to choose more conservative justices, and Democratic presidents tend to choose more liberal justices. Because justices have a lifetime appointment, such appointments can shape the decisions of the Court for many years.

26. The U.S. Supreme Court has original and exclusive jurisdiction over cases in which a state is a party. This exact case was actually brought before the U.S. Supreme Court in 2000. Ultimately, the Court ruled in favor of the state of Maine based on a consent judgment that the two states had signed in 1977, in which they agreed that the border was in the middle of the navigable portion of the Piscataqua River.

27. No. The Supreme Court has absolute discretion over whether it will take cases that come to it by certiorari.

28. *Marbury v. Madison*—The U.S. Supreme Court may review and invalidate laws if they are unconstitutional

Roe v. Wade—A woman's right to an abortion is a privacy right protected by the Fourteenth Amendment.

Brown v. Board of Education—Racial segregation in public schools is unconstitutional.

Texas v. Johnson—Flag burning is "symbolic speech" that is protected by the First Amendment.

Bush v. Gore—The Florida State Supreme Court's order to recount presidential ballots was unconstitutional.

29. Answers will vary.

30. Answers will vary.

31. It is required by the Sixth Amendment of the U.S. Constitution.

32. Michigan and Wisconsin. The conspiracy took place in Michigan, and the act took place in Wisconsin.

33. Donell has committed a misdemeanor and will be fined no more than $2,500 or imprisoned for no more than one year.

34. Answers will vary, but should be supported by a reasoned analysis. Experts argue over what "beyond a reasonable doubt" means, but it certainly means more than just "more likely than not." Black's Law Dictionary defines "reasonable doubt" as "the doubt that prevents one from being firmly convinced of a defendant's guilt."

35. No. The physical act and the mental state were not present at the same time.

36. Crimes against the person include assault, battery, homicide, kidnapping, and sex offenses. Crimes against personal property include larceny, robbery, forgery, embezzlement, and vandalism. Crimes against the home or dwelling include burglary and arson. Crimes against the judicial system include perjury and bribery.

185

Teacher's Guide

37. Carlos has not committed a crime, because it was an accident.

38. No. While he has threatened to inflict injury, he does not have the apparent ability to inflict the injury, and Mike cannot reasonably believe that he is going to be harmed imminently.

39. Yes. But he has not committed an act of criminal homicide.

40. Yes. The killing occurred with malice aforethought, because it was committed with the presence of intent to commit a dangerous felony.

41. Answers will vary, but should be supported by reasoned analysis. Examples that have been determined by courts to be sufficient are (a) when two people suddenly get into a fight and, during the fight, one kills the other; (b) when someone is in fear of his or her own life and kills the person who caused that fear; and (c) when someone finds that his or her spouse has been unfaithful. When the students give their examples, watch out for

scenarios in which the defendant's reaction is unreasonable or in which the defendant should have had time to calm down.

42. Yes. Charlie is guilty of involuntary manslaughter because the killing resulted from the commission of a lawful act done negligently. In fact, if the jurisdiction within which Charlie works considers it a crime to do electrical work without an electrician's license, the killing would have resulted from the commission of an unlawful act other than a dangerous felony.

43. Yes. Because Erik cannot leave or escape, he would be considered detained.

44. He has committed aggravated kidnapping because Philip is a child. Remember that whether or not Philip consented is irrelevant.

45. 1. ASSAULT 2. HOMICIDE 3. KIDNAPPING
    4. MURDER 5. BATTERY

46. No. Sheila does not have the requisite intent to permanently deprive the owner of his interest in the car.

Daily Warm-Ups: Law

47. Carmen has committed embezzlement because she had lawful possession of the coat when she converted it.

48. He or she has committed false pretenses. Larceny involves the taking of possession, but not title.

49. Robbery involves force or the threat of immediate harm.

50. Barry has committed extortion, because the threat of harm was not immediate.

51. No. The ring was not actually stolen. If the ring had actually been stolen, then Percy would be guilty because the circumstances should have put him on notice that it was stolen.

52. Danny and Dawn are both guilty. Danny is guilty because he signed his mother's name to the check, and Dawn is guilty because she knew that it was forged and presented it to the bank anyway.

53. No. The destruction was not intentional.

54. 1. LARCENY 2. EXTORTION 3. ROBBERY 4. FORGERY 5. EMBEZZLEMENT

55. No. Raul has not committed burglary, because he did not intend to commit the crime when he entered the house.

56. Yes. He acted with reckless disregard for an obvious risk. Note that if it was his own home, he could not be convicted of arson.

57. Answers will vary, but should be supported by reasoned analysis.

58. She has not committed perjury because whether or not she likes, loves, or loathes pizza is immaterial to the judicial proceeding.

59. No. Because Geri has not committed perjury, Silvio's inducement for her to lie cannot be considered subornation of perjury.

60. Randy, Donald, and Jose: Randy for accepting the bribe, Donald for encouraging the offer of the bribe, and Jose for offering the bribe.

61. The three who actually entered the bank for the robbery would be principals because they actually committed the offense.

Teacher's Guide

62. Two. The getaway driver and the one who backed out acted as accomplices. Note that even though one person backed out, he or she still aided in the commission of the offense.

63. Answers will vary, but should be supported by reasoned analysis. This is unlikely to be considered sufficient action to prevent the crime.

64. The family members and friends who assisted in keeping the criminals from being arrested acted as accessories after the fact.

65. No. She has merely prepared, but she has not performed an overt act.

66. Neither is guilty of a conspiracy. For a conspiracy to be present, there must be two people who agree to commit a crime and two people who intend that the crime actually be committed. Steve is working for the police and does not intend that the crime actually be committed.

67. Yes. Withdrawal is not a defense to solicitation.

68. Exculpating, because it provides the basis for an acquittal.

69. Answers will vary, but should be supported by reasoned analysis.

70. Answers will vary, but should be supported by reasoned analysis. Imagine how difficult it would be if, in every case, the state had to offer testimony and evidence to prove that the defendant was sane.

71. No.

72. No.

73. Yes.

74. No. Even though she knew it was wrong, she could not control her conduct.

75. Yes. The crime that he would be accused of is assault, which is a specific intent crime. If Fredo can show that his intoxication prevented him from forming the requisite intent, he could be found not guilty of the crime.

76. It was involuntary because the intoxicant was prescribed by a doctor, and Jamie did not know that it could have an intoxicating effect. She will be acquitted because she could not resist the impulse.

Daily Warm-Ups: Law

77. Jason cannot be convicted as an adult for the crime, but he may be punished as a juvenile offender.

78. Answers will vary, but should be supported by reasoned analysis.

79. She can claim it, but she is not going to be successful because she used deadly force to prevent a nondeadly attack.

80. No, because Stella was not in danger of an imminent attack.

81. Answers may vary, but it is most likely that the court would find in Melissa's favor because she was acting to stop the prevention of a felony (burglary) in the home.

82. No. The force was used a day after the taking.

83. No. It is not reasonably necessary for Gregor to assault Chris physically.

84. No. Debbie created the hazard that led to the necessity.

85. Todd can use the duress defense for the charge of driving under the influence because he reasonably feared for his life. He cannot use the duress defense for killing the pedestrian because the duress defense can never be used to excuse a homicide.

86. No. Larceny is a specific intent crime.

87. No. Now, if Laura had just passed a sign that said the speed limit was 60 miles per hour, even if that sign was mistaken, she would have a valid excuse.

88. The defense works in regard to the battery on Jim, but not on Jimmy because Jimmy is a child and lacks capacity to consent. Roger may be able to claim that he was acting in self-defense, however.

89. No, because Susana is a private citizen and not an agent of the government.

90. Students should do this activity only if they have completed Activities 37–53.

Teacher's Guide

involuntary manslaughter—the killing of another that results from "negligence" or from the commission of an unlawful act (other than a dangerous felony)

embezzlement—the fraudulent appropriation of personal property belonging to someone else by someone in lawful possession of the property

kidnapping—the taking of another person without his or her consent, coupled with either movement of that person or hiding that person in a secret location

voluntary manslaughter—murder that has been provoked

91. There are a number of amendments that affect criminal procedure, including the Fourth (unreasonable searches and seizures, requirements for warrants), Fifth (self-incrimination and due process), Sixth (speedy trial, compulsory process, right to face adverse witnesses and assistance of counsel), and Eighth (excessive bail and cruel and unusual punishment).

92. Answers will vary, but should be supported by reasoned analysis.

93. No. The outside of the luggage (where the evidence was located) could be seen by the public.

94. No. Jared has a financial interest in issuing the warrant; he is not neutral and detached.

95. No. They did not search the place specified in the warrant.

96. The knife can be used as evidence because it was in the passenger compartment. The shotgun cannot be used because it was in the trunk. Without a properly issued and executed warrant, the police can only search the area within the arrested person's reach.

97. No. The police are allowed to search any container within the vehicle that might contain the object for which they are searching. A chair cannot fit inside a shoe box.

98. Yes. The police had the right to be on the premises, and the drugs were in plain sight. Further, as possession of marijuana is a crime, the police had probable cause to believe that the pound of marijuana was evidence of a crime.

Daily Warm-Ups: Law

190

99. No. The gardener does not have the authority to consent to the search.

100. Yes. The police have a legitimate basis for stopping Wilma and, because of the tip that they received and her past offenses, have a good reason to suspect that she is armed and dangerous.

101. No. A violation of the leash law is not a serious crime.

102. No. The police had not started their interrogation.

103. The purpose of the exclusionary rule is to deter the police from violating the rights and liberties that were established in the U.S. Constitution.

104. Yes. The police would have eventually discovered the weapon when they executed the search warrant.

105. Answers will vary, but should be supported by reasoned analysis.

106. Answers will vary, but should be supported by reasoned analysis.

107. Either not guilty or *nolo contendere*.

108. Responses will vary, but should be supported by reasoned analysis. An example of a benefit associated with plea bargaining is that it allows cases to move through the courts faster, thereby freeing up the court's docket to handle other matters. An example of an unfortunate consequence is that innocent people occasionally plead guilty because they are afraid of receiving a longer prison term.

109. b

110. No. His judge was not impartial.

111. Yes. The potential of imprisonment for more than six months exists.

112. No. His conviction should be overturned because his counsel was ineffective.

113. No. He had an opportunity to cross-examine Warren at the preliminary hearing.

114. In a tort case arising out of this incident, the primary focus would be to compensate Daniel for

Teacher's Guide

his injury. In a criminal case arising out of this incident, the primary focus would be to punish Elton for his behavior.

115. It is harder to prove guilt beyond a reasonable doubt.

116. Yes. He can demonstrate an act (Lucy moving the ball), intent (she either meant for him to fall or knew with substantial certainty that he would fall) and causation (her act was a substantial factor in making him fall).

117. No. As a goalie, Darren should expect to be hit by the puck. Therefore, his consent is implied, and there is no harmful or offensive touching.

118. Yes. He has the apparent ability to strike Sean and, even though Sean is not concerned for his safety, there is a reasonable apprehension that Jason will actually commit the battery.

119. Yes. Although there is a means of escape, it is unlikely that Dave would know of the means of escape. Even if he did, that means of escape is not exactly reasonable.

120. No. The plaintiff has to actually suffer severe emotional distress.

121. Yes to both. Raj intentionally threw the ball onto Sasha's property (trespass to land) and that act caused damage to Sasha's garden gnome (trespass to chattels).

122. The first example is trespass to chattels because the length of dispossession is fairly short. If the bike were taken for a month, it would be conversion. The answer to the final question is conversion, because although taken for a short time, the property was destroyed.

123. The patient's consent was not valid because of the doctor's misrepresentation about the possibility of suffering vision loss.

124. Winona will prevail because she reasonably believed that she was being attacked and used the amount of force necessary to prevent the attack.

125. Tammy will prevail, because her attack against Winona had concluded, and she was not in a position to launch another attack.

Daily Warm-Ups: Law

126. Quinton's necessity was public (acting to protect the people on the playground). Quinton will prevail and will not be liable for any damages.

127. Tran will prevail. It appears from the facts that Tran would have left if Deborah simply had asked him to leave.

128. Answers will vary, but should be supported by reasoned analysis.

129. Answers will vary, but should be supported by reasoned analysis.

130. Yes. It is reasonable to contemplate that this fan would have been injured by Freddie's conduct.

131. The client will prevail. Because James is a professional accountant, he will be held to a standard of care that requires him to possess and exercise the skill and knowledge that a member of his profession or occupation who is in good standing in his community or a similar community would possess and exercise. Certainly that standard of care would require James to stay abreast of changes in the law.

132. Yes. Even though the fee is small, it is a required

Daily Warm-Ups: Law

fee and, therefore, the passengers are treated as paying passengers.

133. Although the neighbor's son chose Heidi's property to conduct this activity, Heidi was at work and did not know about it. Therefore, it is not reasonable to expect that she could have controlled the neighbor's activity.

134. No. The museum owner expects and intends that people will come to the museum to view the exhibits, not to sell products.

135. Art is a licensee because he has permission to be on the property.

136. Absolutely not. Because she is in violation of the law, she is negligent *per se*.

137. Yes, under the doctrine of *res ipsa loquitur*.

138. Most likely yes, because Alison's behavior (driving while intoxicated) is particularly reckless.

139. Yes. Chandler's injury would not have happened but for Susan's act, and Susan's act was a substantial factor in his injury.

140. Yes. Susan's act set a chain of events in motion

Teacher's Guide

that resulted in a foreseeable harm.

141. Nothing. In a contributory negligence state, if the plaintiff was at all negligent and that negligence contributed to her damages, there is no award.

142. Answers will vary, but should be supported by reasoned analysis.

143. Answers will vary, but should be supported by reasoned analysis.

144. 1. Yes. 2. No. This is not an original work by Rob.

145. No. It is not fixed in a tangible form of expression.

146. Walch Publishing, because the textbook is a "work made for hire."

147. Yes. Anger has the exclusive right to reproduce the work. The web site is distributing copies of the work and, arguably, authorizing others to make copies.

148. It is less likely, because Geoff's use is commercial in nature.

149. Less likely. Although the amount of the portion used is small, the substantiality is considerable, so

the work would be entitled to more protection. Further, the magazine's use had a tremendous impact on the potential market and value of the work.

150. Answers will vary. Point out to students the copyright notice of a book you have in the classroom.

151. No. You cannot maintain a suit for infringement unless you have registered the copyright.

152. It started on January 1, 2005, and ends on January 1, 2120.

153. Yes.

154. No. It is not used in commerce.

155. Yes. They do not have to show actual confusion, just a substantial likelihood of confusion.

156. a design patent

157. Answers will vary, but should demonstrate a comprehension of the requirements that the invention be both new and useful.

158. No. The improvement is obvious.

159. The company has to get Gavin to transfer or

assign his interest in the invention. Typically, employers make their employees sign an assignment of rights in all things that they invent during the course of their employment when they are first hired.

160. No. The patent right gives her the ability to prevent someone else from selling her invention, but it does not give her the right to sell it.

161. Roald could enter into a license agreement with Henry under which Henry could continue to use the invention and Roald would be compensated.

162. No. He has not marked his invention properly. He can only get damages after he has notified Sven of the infringement and Sven continues to infringe.

163. No. The company has not taken reasonable precautions to keep the recipe a secret.

164. Answers will vary, but should be supported by reasoned analysis.

165. No. Child support payments are not discharged in bankruptcy.

166. Chapter 9

167. Yes. The eight-year restriction is counted from the date that the debtor filed his or her original petition. In this case, Walter would have been allowed to file for another Chapter 7 bankruptcy on March 1, 2014.

168. Students should do this activity only after they have completed Activity 167. In a Chapter 7 case, most debts are discharged in exchange for the surrender of property, while the goal of a Chapter 11 case is to reorganize debt so that it is more manageable. Also, an independent trustee is appointed to manage the Chapter 7 case, while the debtor (as the debtor in possession) manages the Chapter 11 case.

169. Answers will vary, but should be supported by reasoned analysis.

170. Most likely not, because the marriage was not valid in Alabama.

171. No. Both parties must want to be married, and Octavio, at least, does not.

Teacher's Guide

172. Yes. A no-fault divorce jurisdiction does not require a showing of wrongdoing. The existence of irreconcilable differences is sufficient.

173. Answers will vary, but should be supported by reasoned analysis.

174. Answers will vary, but should be supported by reasoned analysis.

175. Answers will vary, but should be supported by reasoned analysis. Essentially, if a court thinks that a couple can work together sufficiently to share physical custody, it is unlikely that the court would find that they cannot work together to resolve issues in legal custody. Further, if both parties share physical custody, but only one can make important decisions, it would promote tension and make one parent subject to the will of the other.

176. Answers will vary, but should be supported by reasoned analysis.

177. Answers will vary, but should be supported by reasoned analysis.

178. There are six sections. This question would have been in the reading comprehension section.

179. Answers will vary, but should be supported by reasoned analysis.

180. Answers will vary, but should be supported by reasoned analysis. Knowledge of the U.S. Constitution and the legislative process would be useful to politicians. Knowledge of criminal law and criminal procedure would be useful in law enforcement. The FBI actually hires many of its agents right out of law school. There is a great demand for journalists who can serve as legal analysts. These journalists cover matters ranging from criminal and civil trials to reporting on developments in the United States Congress.

Turn downtime into learning time!

Other books in the

Daily Warm-Ups series:

- Algebra
- Algebra II
- Analogies
- Art
- Biology
- Character Education
- Chemistry
- Common English Idioms
- Commonly Confused Words
- Critical Thinking
- Daily Edits
- Earth Science

- Everyday Skills
- Figurative Language
- Geography
- Geometry
- Journal Writing
- Logic
- Math Brain Teasers
- Math Word Problems
- Mythology
- Physics
- Poetry
- Pre-Algebra

- Prefixes, Suffixes, & Roots
- Shakespeare
- Spelling & Grammar
- Test-Prep Words
- U.S. History
- Vocabulary
- World Cultures
- World History
- World Religions
- Writing